I0210632

Story Share

Gospel Story-arc Evangelism Training

Story Share

Gospel Story-arc Evangelism Training

Randal Gilmore

EXALT Publications
Fishers, IN

Copyright © 2025 Randal L. Gilmore

All Rights Reserved

Scripture quotations are from the ESV® Bible (The Holy Bible, English Standard Version®), copyright © 2001 by Crossway, a publishing ministry of Good News Publishers. Used by permission. All rights reserved.

ISBN: 978-1-965465-01-1

Content

Foreword

WHY GOSPEL STORY-ARC® MESSAGING

Countless people live in complete ignorance of who Jesus is. Others recognize His name but know very little of His story. Still others fill in the gaps with their own thoughts and impressions—crafting a "personal" version of Jesus, as if He were a religious Build-A-Bear®.

In the past, our gospel presentations have relied on familiar frameworks—acrostics like the ABCs of Salvation or logical outlines like the Romans Road. While these can be effective, they are not foolproof.

Why?

Because of their bias for **message efficiency**.

They are short, simple, and easy to remember by design. But brevity comes at a cost. The fuller story gets left out. And when the story is incomplete, listeners "fill in the blanks" with whatever they already know—or think they know—about Jesus.

That's called pre-existing knowledge. And here's the problem: when it's mistaken, or missing altogether, a heart-deep profession of faith becomes far more difficult.

Younger generations in the West are a clear example of this. According to the Barna Group and their report on Gen Z, only 4% of those born after 1999 hold a

Christian worldview. The Barna Report on "Reviving Evangelism" adds, "It's safe to say that the assumption that most people have been raised with similar faith practices or even a common religious language is already outdated." This means we can't assume people share even the basic foundation needed to make sense of a partial gospel message.

And logic alone won't fix it.

The postmodern mind rejects logical reasoning applied to religion. In some cultures, religion has never been about logic—postmodern or not. Think of the builders of Babel. They were rational when designing the tower, yet irrational on matters of faith. Other ways of thinking took over. It's what allowed them to believe a man-made tower could reach into heaven and bring down its blessings.

So, what do we do?

We turn to what God Himself has given us: **the power of story**.

Gospel Story-arc® messaging uses the dynamics of story to overcome these barriers. In his book, *Story Smart: Using the Science of Story to Persuade, Influence, Inspire, and Teach*, story expert, Kendal Haven, summarizes the research that confirms what Scripture has shown all along—story is the best way to provide context and relevance in any kind of communication.

Haven calls story "the interstate carpool lane into the mind." And that makes sense, because story is part of God's design for how our minds work. And for how He reveals Jesus to us in Scripture.

We love to tell Jesus' story because of who He is: the Christ, the Son of God, the Lord of all, and coming King of kings. So we're passionate about Gospel Story-arc® messaging that proclaims these and other truths about Him.

We also tell Jesus' story because He deserves better than for countless people—even entire nations—to live in unbelief and ignorance of His teaching, His death and resurrection, His promised return, and the worldview He lived and died to restore.

Jesus deserves better.

GOSPEL STORY-ARC® EVANGELISM TRAINING AND RESOURCES

For more training and resources, visit gospelstoryarc.org. There you'll find the audio version of this course—including a live recording of the messaging shared with an audience. You can also order the Gospel Story-arc® Cubes and Tracts, which unfold to tell Jesus' story using the same pictures featured in Lessons 3–10.

HOW TO USE THIS RESOURCE

This resource will show you how to use Gospel Story-arc messaging to share your faith in Jesus. The messaging has been crafted to summarize Jesus' story in Scripture with accuracy, using what we know from science about story structure.

This resource is divided into 12 lessons:

Lesson 1: An Introduction to Story

Lesson 2: Overview of Gospel Story-arc™ Messaging

Lessons 3-10: Gospel Story-arc® Messaging

Lessons 11-12: How to Begin Gospel Conversations, Parts 1 and 2

Bonus Material on Evangelism Best Practices, Gospel Story-arc® Philosophy, and Gospel Story-arc® Messaging Re: Worldviews of Honor/Shame, Innocence/Guilt, and Love/Fear.

EXPECTED OUTCOMES

By the end of this training, you should be able to:

- **Tell Jesus' story with clarity and confidence** using the seven-part story-arc framework—without collapsing the gospel into a list of isolated truths or a single climax moment.

- **Lead with story rather than argument**, using the messaging as a frame that helps listeners make sense of everything else you may share later.

- **Use the Gospel Story-arc® Cube or Tract with fluency**, matching each panel to its corresponding story movement.

- **Engage real people in gospel conversations**, with practical ways to start, sustain, and navigate your way through.

- **Handle common interruptions with calm confidence**, deferring deeper questions when needed and drawing on "Going Deeper" content as your knowledge grows.

- **Build spiritual and relational courage**—not just memorized phrasing—so that your evangelism becomes both faithful and natural.

These outcomes reflect a simple hope: that you will become a "Jesus-storyteller" who helps others meet the real Jesus—the Jesus whose story fills the Scriptures.

A PRACTICE RHYTHM THAT BUILDS SPIRITUAL MUSCLE MEMORY

The effectiveness of this training hinges on a steady rhythm of repetition and relational practice. The goal is not only familiarity with the words, but confidence in telling the story with warmth, accuracy, and heart. So, consider this simple pattern:

Daily (10–15 minutes):

- Read the messaging aloud two to three times per day, letting the flow of the story shape your instincts.
- If you can, read with the Cube or Tract open, matching each panel to the words you're speaking.

Twice Weekly (15–20 minutes):

- Practice with a partner.
- Take turns telling the story with the Cube.
- Correct one another with kindness, aiming for growth in clarity and confidence.

Weekly (30 minutes):

- Review one "Going Deeper" section.
- Choose one real-world application question:
- Where would I pause for connection?
- Which worldview doorway might this person be living in—shame, guilt, or fear?

Monthly:

- Share the messaging in a real conversation when the opportunity arises.
- Reflect on what felt natural, what felt stiff, and what you want to strengthen next.

This rhythm supports a key principle: **Imitate Before You Innovate**. Attempt to memorize the messaging as presented here. You can always adapt your wording in the future, but first let the story settle into your mind and heart.

GETTING THE MOST OUT OF THIS RESOURCE

Follow these practical steps to gain more from this resource:

1. **Practice using the Gospel Story-arc™ Cube or Pamphlet as you read, matching the illustrations on each panel to the content it represents.**

2. **Practice with a partner.**

3. **Stick with the wording.**

   The messaging presented in this resource leverages the science of story for maximum effectiveness. Stick to it for now. You can always adapt your wording in the future as you share. But for now, the wording you've been given will build "spiritual muscle memory" and weaken the temptation to reduce the gospel to a single climax point—which is what can happen with gospel acrostics and logical formulas.

   Remember, Gospel Story-arc® messaging is not intended to be the only information we share about Jesus and the Bible. It's the messaging we lead with. It sets the frame and provides context for everything else.

4. **Learn the content in each Going Deeper section.**

   The Going Deeper sections are summaries of content we teach elsewhere in the Gospel Story-arc Bible Study and Discipleship. It's included here to give you an even fuller understanding of the story told about Jesus in Scripture.

5. **Use the page margins for notes.**

6. **Access the audio version of this training online to review the teaching as often as you wish (https://gospelstoryarc.org).**

7. **Access the Gospel Story-arc Community to find even more resources and encouragement:**

Lesson 1

An Introduction to Story

The word "story" is like an ordinary cardboard box, like one you might buy at The Container Store®. You can fill it with almost anything, and no one will object. It's why the word "story" has so many different meanings. Inside we might find an epic, or some tale reduced to a few lines. We might find an account that's totally true, or totally a yarn. We might find a narrative carefully crafted to evoke a particular effect, or one told off the cuff.

In the case of Gospel Story-arc™ messaging, the word "story" refers to the narrative of Scripture as a true, historical, and carefully-crafted epic account of Jesus Christ, the Son of God, a narrative empowered to bring people to faith in him.

Obviously, it's not possible to share the entire story of Jesus every time we engage in gospel conversations. We must choose which content to include and which to exclude. The choices we make in Gospel Story-arc™ messaging flow from our application of the science of story.

Research into the use of story highlights the influential power of narratives that include the following elements:

- a character
- a character's goal
- a motive that makes the character's goal important
- an antagonist or obstacle blocking the character's success
- the likelihood or not of whether the character will succeed (how much of a threat is the antagonist; how significant is the obstacle)
- consequences of the character not reaching his or her goal (the more danger, the better)
- a coherent arrangement of the events that tell what happens

There are many ways to arrange a story's elements, so that the story makes sense. One of the simplest is with a beginning, a middle, and an end See chart below). A more sophisticated arrangement expands beginning, middle, and end into seven sections: exposition, inciting incident, rising action, climax, falling action, resolution, and untying (see chart on page 20).

Simple	More Sophisticated
Beginning	*Exposition*
	Inciting Incident
Middle	*Rising Action*
	Climax
	Falling Action
End	*Resolution*
	Untying

This seven-fold structure forms what we mean by a "story-arc." A "story-arc" starts at the beginning of a story and goes to the end, but it rises above the events of a story's timeline, so people can better visualize and understand what a story is about.

Gospel Story-arc™ messaging combines the elements of story with a "story-arc" to summarize the epic biblical account of who Jesus is, what Jesus did, who we are, and the call to believe. The chart on page 16 lays this out. The graphic below it shows the seven-fold structure of a story-arc overlaying a depiction of Jesus on the road to Emmaus, recalling that:

> beginning with Moses and all the Prophets, he interpreted to them in all the Scriptures the things concerning himself. (Luke 24:27)

Jesus' own telling of his story is biblical warrant for the approach we take with Gospel Story-arc™ messaging. Our desire is for people to believe in Jesus, with their hearts fully engaged, just as those early disciples responded when they heard his story directly from him:

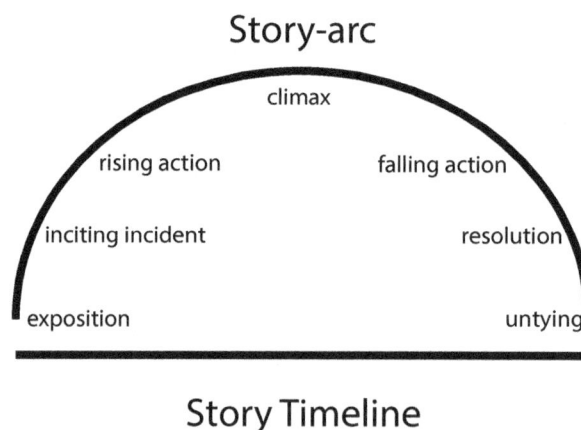

Story-arc

climax

rising action   falling action

inciting incident   resolution

exposition   untying

Story Timeline

Did not our hearts burn within us while he talked to us on the road, while he opened the Scriptures? (Luke 24:32)

A More Sophisticated Arrangement of Story Structure

Simple	More Sophisticated		
Beginning	Exposition		Panel 1 - The God of the Bible...
			Panel 2 - God created Adam and Eve...
	Inciting Incident		Panel 3 - Soon an enemy spirit called...
			Panel 4 - In response, God announced...
			Panel 5 - The hostility between the...
Middle	Rising Action		Panel 6 - Over time, God revealed more...
	Climax		Panel 6 - Eventually Jesus came into the world...
	Falling Action		Panel 7 - Jesus remains seated for now...
End	Resolution Untying		Panel 7 - Someday Jesus will return...

Lesson 2

An Overview of Gospel Story-arc Messaging

PRACTICE (READ ONLY)

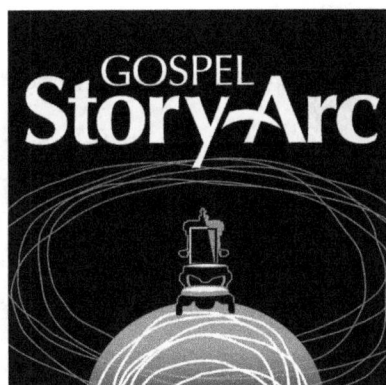

Jesus' story begins with the God of the Bible, the only true God, a great Creator and King whose nature is love.

This is the opening line:

"In the beginning, God created the heaven and the earth."

God created heaven and earth to be places where his rule would be fully honored and obeyed.

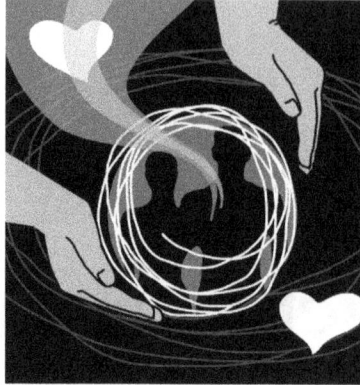

God created Adam and Eve, the first humans, and blessed them with four types of perfect relationships: with Him, with each other, with self, and with the rest of creation.

When God finished, he saw all that he made and blessed it, and he said it was "very good."

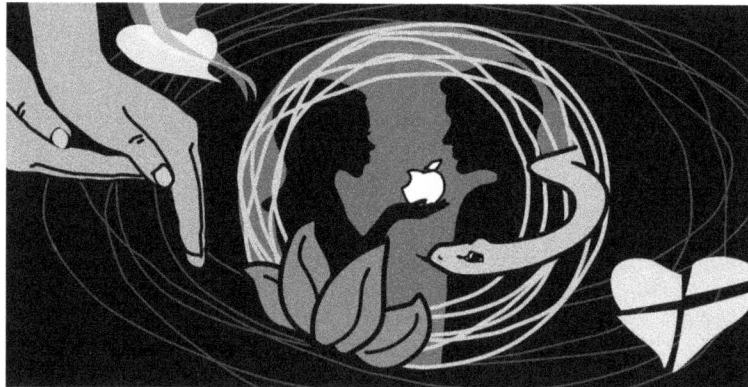

Soon an enemy spirit called Satan came into the world to steal, kill, and destroy. Using a serpent, he tempted Adam and Eve to rebel against God. Adam and Eve gave into the temptation and disobeyed. As a result, the four types of perfect relationships were broken. Before this, there was honor, innocence, and love; now there is shame, guilt, and fear.

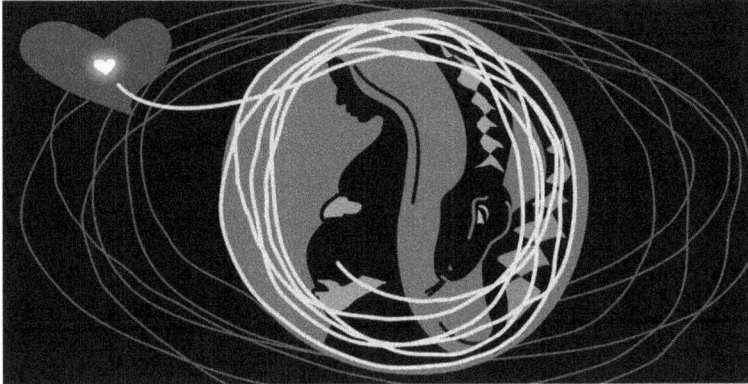

In response, God announced curses on the serpent, on Adam and Eve, and on the ground. The earth was no longer "very good." Sin and death became part of the world, along with pain, suffering, evil, and unbelief.

Still, there was hope. As part of the curse on the serpent, God said he would put hostility between it and the woman, and between "the seed of the serpent" and someone called "the seed of the woman." The expression, "seed of the woman," points to a Savior who would be born in an unusual way. His father would not be a man. Instead, he would be born of a virgin, and God would be his father. Since God would be his father, "the seed of the woman" would have both the nature of God and the nature of man.

The hostility between the serpent and "the seed of the woman" divided humanity into two sides going forward—the side of the serpent vs. the side of "the seed of the woman."

God promised that someday there would be an epic conflict between the serpent and "the seed of the woman." God said that the serpent would "bruise" the heel of "the seed of the woman," causing him to experience pain and suffering.

But God also said that "the seed of the woman" would "bruise" the head of the serpent, indicating that "the seed of the woman" will win the epic conflict. (When you "bruise" the head of a serpent, the serpent loses!)

The victory of "the seed of the woman" indicates he is also the Savior. He will rescue people from the side of the serpent and someday restore all things. Meanwhile, the serpent will do everything he can to deny "the seed of the woman" space in the world.

At the end of God's promise, one question remained: **Who is the seed of the woman?**

Over many years, God revealed more about the character and family line of "the seed of the woman." He also revealed the circumstances of the Savior's birth, and the miracles he would perform to prove his identity. Eventually, Jesus came into the world as the promised "seed of the woman." Born of a virgin, Jesus grew into adulthood and lived a perfect life. He also performed many miracles.

But the people of Jesus' day rejected him and murdered him on a cross. Jesus died willingly, knowing that his suffering and death was the "bruising of the heel" predicted earlier. Jesus also knew his death would pay the penalty people deserve for joining in the rebellion against God. Jesus spoke of his great love as motivation for dying to pay for our sin and rebellion, saying:

> "Greater love hath no man than this, that a man lay down his life for his friends."
> John 15:13

After three days, Jesus rose to new life in power and victory over sin and death. His resurrection marked the beginning of "the crushing of the serpent's head.

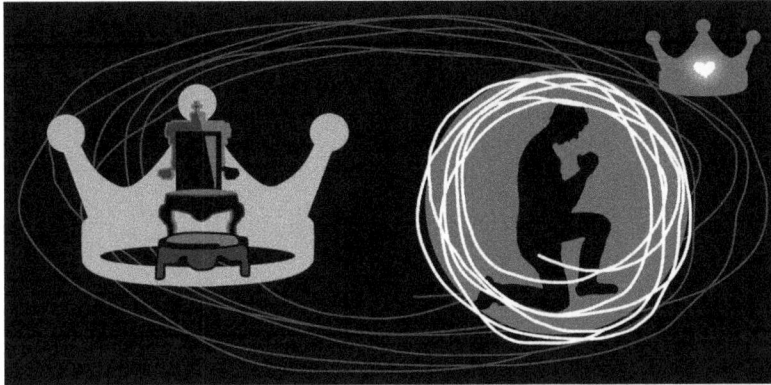

Forty days later, Jesus ascended into heaven and sat down at the right hand of God to be exalted as King of kings and Lord of lords.

Jesus remains seated for now at the right hand of God the Father, where he is interceding for us as our high priest, and building his Church, calling people from every nation to believe in him.

Someday Jesus will return to judge the earth for its sin and unbelief. At that time, "every knee will bow and every tongue will confess that Jesus is Lord." But it will be too late for people who refused to believe on Jesus in this life. They will be punished and separated from God forever.

Now, it is still possible for people to be saved from sin, brokenness, and judgment through faith in Jesus. Jesus said:

> "For God so loved the world, that he gave his only begotten Son, that whosoever believeth in him should not perish, but have everlasting life."
> John 3:16

Through faith in Jesus, we are forgiven and our relationships to God are restored. Jesus completes the restoration of all things after the final judgment. Then everything will begin again in the new heaven and new earth under God's rule.

What is your heart telling you now to believe about Jesus?

Lesson 3

The God of the Bible...

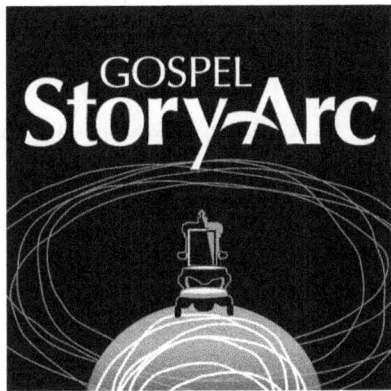

PRACTICE AND MEMORIZE — PANEL 1

The God of the Bible is a great Creator and King whose nature is love.

"In the beginning, God created the heavens and the earth" to be places where his rule was fully honored and obeyed.

God also sent his Spirit into the world to interact with the material world.

GOING DEEPER

Gospel Story-arc™ messaging does not start with proof that God exists. Similar to Genesis 1:1, the messaging simply asserts that God exists as both a great Creator and King:

The God of the Bible is a great Creator and King.

Many Christians think they must prove that God exists before they can start sharing the gospel. They also believe they need to prove that the Bible is God's Word; that the theory of evolution is wrong; that God is holy; that humans are sinful, etc. The Gospel Story-arc™ Project is unequivocally committed to these truths. But our first concern is to tell the Bible's story of Jesus. So we begin with telling, not arguing. Apologetics may prove necessary in time, after we set the frame by telling the Bible's story. Many people will inquire about the existence of God, creationism, Noah's flood, and resurrection from the dead. So we must be prepared to give an answer. But the story comes first.

GOD IS A GREAT KING

In the opening lines of Gospel Story-arc™ messaging, we also assert one of the primary reasons why God created the heavens and the earth:

In the beginning, God created the heavens and the earth to be places where his rule is fully honored and obeyed.

Even though Genesis 1 does not mention the word "King," it doesn't take long to figure out that "King" is part of God's identity. The Scriptures show throughout that God is the prototype of all kings. Consider these example texts:

(1) Genesis 14:22 — "But Abram said to the king of Sodom, 'I have lifted my hand to the Lord, God Most High, the Possessor of heaven and earth...'" God is an even greater king than the king of Sodom. The king of Sodom ruled over a tiny city; God rules over heaven and earth.

(2) Proverbs 21:1 — "The king's heart is a stream of water in the hand of the Lord; he turns it wherever he will." Earthly kings represent some of the most self-willed people on the earth, and yet God is sovereign over them. He turns their hearts in whatever direction he pleases. God's ability to rule over the hearts

of self-willed earthly kings indicates that he also has the ability also to rule over those who are not so strong-willed—in other words, God has the ability to rule over everyone.

(3) Psalm 22:28 — "For kingship belongs to the Lord, and he rules over the nations." Once again, God's kingdom is not limited to a single nation.

(4) Psalm 47:2 — "For the Lord, the Most High, is to be feared, a great king over all the earth." Everyone on earth is to reverence God as King.

(5) Psalm 95:3 — "For the Lord is a great God, and a great King above all gods." God is the ruler also over all lesser spiritual powers.

(6) Psalm 103:19 — "The Lord has established his throne in the heavens, and his kingdom rules over all." Among other things, God's kingdom is not limited to the earth. God rules over the sun, moon, and stars too!

(7) Psalm 145:13 — "Your kingdom is an everlasting kingdom, and your dominion endures throughout all generations." God's kingdom never comes to an end. God continues to be King in our day. His rule includes our generation.

Kings are rulers who possess sovereign power and authority. Their kingdoms are the realms over which rule. Today, few countries are governed by kings or queens. Most govern themselves in another way. For countries that still have royal families, their kings and queens have become figurehead leaders. In contrast, God's role as King has never changed. He remains king over all and his rule is from everlasting to everlasting. He rules with power and authority over the entire universe.

The expression "Kingdom of God" can refer broadly to God's universal rule. It can also refer more narrowly to Christ's here on the earth; which is takes place at the end of the story as Panel #7 shows:

> Someday, Jesus will return to judge the earth for its sin and un-
> belief. At that time, "every knee will bow and every tongue will
> confess that Jesus is Lord"; in other words, that he is the Savior
> and Restorer that God promised to send. But it will be too late
> for people who refused to believe in Jesus in this life. They will be

punished and separated from God forever.

Meanwhile, it is still possible for people to be saved from sin, brokenness, and judgment through faith in Jesus. Jesus said: "For God so loved the world, that he gave his only Son, that whoever believes in him should not perish but have eternal life."

Through faith in Jesus, Christians are forgiven and begin to experience restoration of the four broken relationships; though only in part for now. The promised restoration of all things will be completed after the final judgment; when Jesus delivers his kingdom to God the Father and everything begins again in the new heaven and new earth under God's rule.

GOD'S SPIRIT

The last statement included under Panel #1 is about God's Spirit:

God also sent his Spirit into the world to interact with the material world.

This statement is based on Genesis 1:2:

"And the Spirit of God was hovering over the face of the waters."

The word "hovering" means "to flutter." The same word appears in Deuteronomy 32:11-12. There it stands for the care an adult eagle provides for its young, as it "flutters" over its nest:

Like an eagle that stirs up its nest, that flutters over its young, spreading out its wings, catching them, bearing them on its pinions, the Lord alone guided him, no foreign god was with him.

It's easy to imagine an eagle stirring up its nest, fluttering to bring its sleeping chicks to life; the exact word picture we're supposed to imagine, as the Spirit of God stirs up the "nest" of creation. The rest of Genesis 1 follows as a consequence of the Spirit's fluttering. In the end, the Spirit's fluttering also points to the reality of the spirit world. The spirit world is active in the physical realm from the start; setting the stage for the rival spirit to enter, and then animate a serpent to incite rebellion against God.

Lesson 4

God created Adam and Eve...

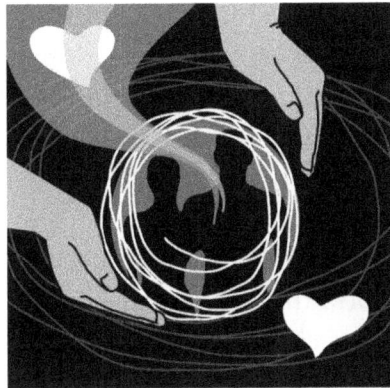

PRACTICE AND MEMORIZE — PANEL 2

God created Adam and Eve, the first humans, in his image, and blessed them with four types of perfect relationships: with Him, with each other, with self, and with the rest of creation.*

When God finished creating, he saw all that he made and blessed it, and said it was "very good."

GOING DEEPER

Let's look more closely at the four types of perfect relationships with which God blessed the first human beings:

- Relationship with God — A perfect relationship with God would mean not having any sin in your life; and always believing in God, always trusting him, honoring him, and doing his will; always glad to see him, and having him as a close friend.

- Relationship with Others — A perfect relationship would mean never getting into any arguments or fights with anyone, always living in perfect harmony with everyone, always loving them, and vice versa.

- Relationship with Self — A perfect relationship with self would mean not ever having feelings of shame or guilt; not from a lack of conscience; but because you never do anything wrong. You never do anything that disappoints yourself.

- Relationship with Creation — A perfect relationship with creation would mean living in a world that is completely safe and never dangerous, full of good and never evil, rich with resources, and no obstacles hindering your ability to be manage them—all for God's glory and your good.

HUMAN EXCEPTIONALISM

Genesis 1:26-27 says:

> Then God said, "'Let us make man in our image, after our likeness. And let them have dominion over the fish of the sea and over the birds of the heavens and over the livestock and over all the earth and over every creeping thing that creeps on the earth.' So God created man in his own image, in the image of God he created him; male and female, he created them."

Human beings are not just another type of animal. We are the only creatures God made in his image and commissioned to represent him to the rest of creation.

Bible teachers disagree on the meaning of "made in the image of God"; though some parts of it are obvious. God made both male and female in his image, indicating their equality before him, and showering both with his love. God's love makes it possible for us to connect God's image and commission to all four types of perfect relationships.

At its core, God's love always involves honoring someone as a person and providing for their good. So God loved the first humans by honoring them with his image and commission, providing for their good, and giving them purpose and meaning.

God's image and commission gave the first humans an opportunity to love him back, to honor him as their Creator and King, to put their faith in him, to obey him, and to find hope in his blessing.

God's image and commission also offered the first humans an opportunity to love each other as God loved them; to honor others as bearers of God's image, also charged to do God's will; to provide for mutual good; and to help each other obey.

Finally, God's image and commission provided the first humans with the opportunity to love themselves in a way that is proper, absent of any undue pride or shame.

WHY WE INCLUDE THE FOUR RELATIONSHIPS IN GOSPEL STORY-ARC™ MESSAGING

Whenever and wherever Gospel Story-arc™ messaging is shared, people connect on a heart level to hearing about the four relationships.

In addition, we include the four relationships in the messaging...

- Because they help people to understand what's unique about human beings compared to the rest of creation.

- Because they tie directly to the meaning of life on many levels; providing on-ramps to connect with the rest of Jesus' story.

- Because they add meaning to the END of the story. That's the part we call the UNTYING, when God creates the new heavens and new earth. At that time, God restores all four of the relationships to perfection. When we get there, you'll see how the Book of Revelation describes this.

Lesson 5

Soon a rival spirit...

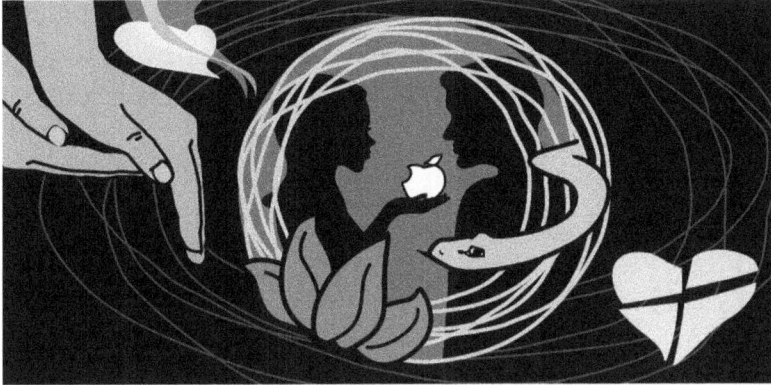

PRACTICE AND MEMORIZE — PANEL 3

Soon an enemy spirit called Satan entered the world. Satan used a serpent to tempt Adam and Eve to rebel against God.

Adam and Eve gave into the temptation and disobeyed. As a consequence, the four types of perfect relationships became broken. Where once there was honor, innocence, and love, now there was shame, guilt, and fear.

GOING DEEPER

Genesis 3:1-7 tells what happened when an enemy spirit took control of a serpent and incited Adam and Eve to rebel against God:

> Now the serpent was more crafty than any other beast of the field that the LORD God had made. He said to the woman, "Did God actually say, 'You shall not eat of any tree in the garden'?" And the woman said to the serpent, "We may eat of the fruit of the trees in the garden, but God said, 'You shall not eat of the fruit of the tree that is in the midst of the garden, neither shall you touch it, lest you die.'" But the serpent said to the woman, "You will not surely die. For God knows that when you eat of it your eyes will be opened, and you will be like God, knowing good and evil." So when the woman saw that the tree was good for food, and that it was a delight to the eyes, and that the tree was to be desired to make one wise, she took of its fruit and ate, and she also gave some to her husband who was with her, and he ate. Then the eyes of both were opened, and they knew that they were naked. And they sewed fig leaves together and made themselves loincloths.

Earlier, God gave Adam and Eve this rule:

> "And the Lord God commanded the man, saying, 'You may surely eat of every tree of the garden, but of the tree of the knowledge of good and evil you shall not eat, for in the day that you eat of it you shall surely die.'"

God had blessed Adam and Eve with innocence. They had no firsthand knowledge of evil, and God intended for it to stay that way. He meant for their knowledge of evil to come through him. He did not intend for Adam and Eve to experience evil for themselves. But the rival spirit used a serpent to cast doubt on God's goodness, suggesting that God was a tyrant, and that the restrictions he placed on them were severe and unreasonable:

> "Did God actually say, 'You shall not eat of any tree in the garden?'" (Genesis 3:1)

The woman took the bait, and agreed with the sentiment the serpent offered, that God's prohibition might be overly restrictive:

"We may eat of the fruit of the trees in the garden, but God said,
'You shall not eat of the fruit of the tree that is in the midst of the
garden, neither shall you touch it, lest you die.'" (Genesis 3:3)

God did not say, "neither shall you touch it." By adding this restriction, the
woman showed she was open to further discussion, perhaps even curious about
what God might be withholding from them. The serpent moved in for the kill.

"You will not surely die. For God knows that when you eat of it
your eyes will be opened, and you will be like God, knowing good
and evil." (Genesis 3:5)

Then the serpent lied:

"You will not surely die."

It is the biggest lie ever told. It stands, along with all of Satan's other lies,
behind the error in every philosophy, worldview, or religion that opposes God's
story. When Jesus spoke of it according to John 8, he minced no words:

"He [Satan, the enemy spirit] was a murderer from the beginning,
and has nothing to do with the truth, because there is no truth in
him. When he lies, he speaks out of his own character, for he is a
liar and the father of lies." (John 8:44)

By contrast, Jesus said of himself:

"I am the way, the truth, and the life. No one comes to the Father,
except through me." (John 14:6)

After lying outright, the serpent deceitfully repackaged the consequences of
disobedience as an advantage:

"For God knows that when you eat of it your eyes will be opened,
and you will be like God, knowing good and evil." (Genesis 3:5)

These words imply that God is not a good and wise Creator; that he withheld
something good from Adam and Eve. Eve swallowed the lie and ate from the tree.

Then, " ... she gave some to her husband who was with her, and he ate." (Genesis 3:6) Later in the story, we are told that Adam was not deceived. He deliberately chose to eat from the tree in rebellion against God.

THE SENTENCE OF DEATH

When God commanded Adam and Eve not to eat from the tree of the knowledge of good and evil, he issued a warning:

> "For in the day that you eat of it you shall surely die." (Genesis 2:17)

It turns out that "death" meant more than just physical death. It also meant the death of the four types of perfect relationships. First, the death of their relationship with self:

> "Then the eyes of both were opened, and they knew that they were naked. And they sewed fig leaves together and made themselves loincloths." (Genesis 3:7)

Previously, Adam and Eve "were both naked and not ashamed" (Genesis 2:24). But after their fall, the glory once reflected in their bodies gave way to shame, made obvious by their nakedness.

The second type of death in the story is the death of their relationships with God:

> "And they heard the sound of the Lord God walking in the garden in the cool of the day, and the man and his wife hid themselves from the presence of the Lord God among the trees of the garden." (Genesis 3:9)

These words imply that Adam and Eve were accustomed to interacting openly with God in the garden, but now they hid. When God "finds" them, Adam confesses:

> "I heard the sound of you in the garden, and I was afraid, and I was naked, and I hid myself." (Genesis 3:10)

Previously, Adam and Eve had no reason to fear God. Now that they dishonored God and broke their relationships with him, they lived in fear.

The third type of death is the death of their relationships with each other. In response to God asking if he had eaten from the forbidden tree, Adam said,

> "The woman whom you gave to be with me, she gave me fruit of the tree, and I ate."

Adam blamed Eve, willing to let her suffer the punishment of death, but hoping that he might avoid it. Adam had honored Eve with a hymn of praise after God brought her to him; now, he brushes aside their oneness and suggests that God should spare him and punish only her. Obviously, their relationship was broken.

EXPERIENCING BROKENNESS

Everyone experiences the pain of sin and brokenness; alienation; and frustration of a world gone awry. Just not in the same way. For some, the brokenness of their relationship with God consumes them. For others, it's their relationships with others, or with self, or with the rest of creation. A broken relationship with God should be of primary concern to everyone. But our messaging must allow for other types of brokenness to stand out.

Countless people do not believe in God; especially the God of the Bible. Or they know nothing about him. They haven't developed a sense of guilt over having offended God. Still, they hold brokenness in their hearts. They feel empty and alone, or frustrated and in pain, not in relation to God, but other types of relationships. It's possible to go through one of these other types of brokenness initially to connect Jesus' story to their hearts. This is why the messaging mentions shame, guilt, and fear in opposition to honor, innocence, and love. These represent different worldviews. The messaging allows us to adapt to one of these without changing Jesus' story.

You'll find more detail about these things in a bonus session on "Gospel Story-arc™ Evangelism and Worldview." There, we even suggest pausing at the end of the messaging for Cube Panel 3 to ask:

> "Which of these (referring now to shame, guilt, and fear)—which of these do you think is the most devastating?"

This question could be what it takes to surface the pain, frustration, and alienation tied to their personal experiences with brokenness.

Lesson 6

God makes a promise...

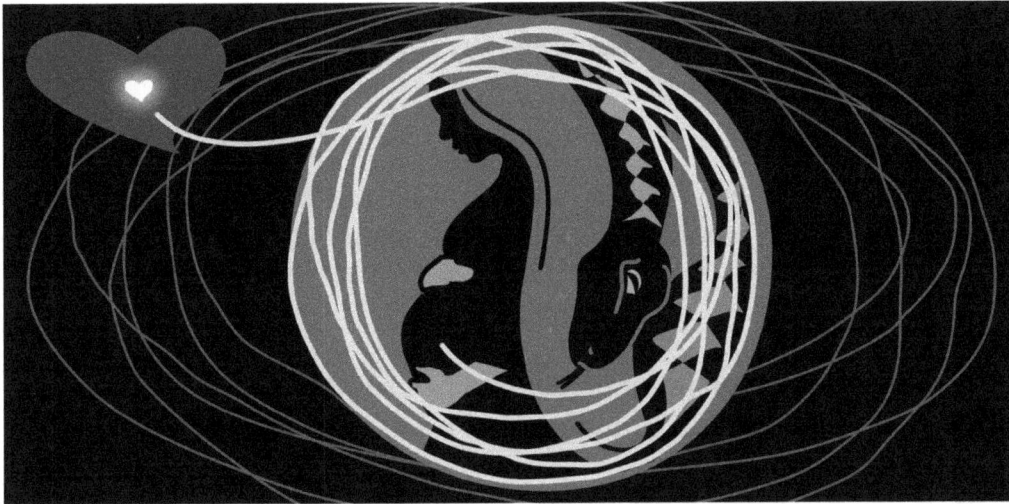

PRACTICE AND MEMORIZE — PANEL 4

In response, God announced curses on the serpent, on Adam and Eve, and on the ground. The earth was no longer "very good." Sin and death became part of the world, as did pain, suffering, evil, and unbelief.

Still, there was hope. As part of the curse on the serpent, God promised to put hostility between it and the woman, and between "the seed of the serpent" and "the seed of the woman." The expression, "seed of the woman," points to a Savior who would be born in an unusual way. No man would be his father. Instead, he will be born of a virgin, and God will be his father. Since God is his father, "the seed of the woman" will have both the nature of God and the nature of man.

GOING DEEPER

The messaging for Panel 4 forms part of the inciting incident of Jesus' story and is based on Genesis 3:15:

> "I will put enmity between you [the rival spirit] and the woman,
> and between your seed and her seed; he shall bruise your head,
> and you [the rival spirit] shall bruise his heel." (Genesis 3:15)

God made this promise in response to the rebellion, in connection to his announcing four broad curses:

(1) against the serpent, that it would be cursed above all livestock and beasts of the field, and that it would be forced to crawl on its belly and eat dust all of its days—Genesis 3:14-15

(2) against the woman in childbirth, and in relationship with her husband; that she would experience pain, and bear the brunt of the disruption of marital roles—Genesis 3:16

(3) against the man, that he would experience pain and deprivation in relation to his struggle for the provisions of life, and that ultimately his physical body would die and return to dust—Genesis 3:17-19

(4) against creation, that it would rebel against man's effort to produce food from it, that some of what it produced would be useless and reasons for more struggle and pain—Genesis 3:17-19

These curses paint an even fuller picture of what God meant when he threatened death as a consequence of rebelling against him. Adam and Eve's disobedience brought radical change to the world; a world God previously blessed and pronounced "very good." Thus, the messaging states:

> The earth was no longer "very good." Sin and death became part of the world, as did pain, suffering, evil, and unbelief.

Skeptics wonder why suffering and evil exist in the world. They believe suffering and evil argue against the existence of God. But just the opposite is true. The curses were intended to call us back to God. If the consequences of rebellion were not severe, or if they were entirely under our control, we wouldn't pay attention. We would deceive ourselves into believing that we don't need God or the restoration he promises. So God, in his grace, uses our exposure to brokenness, pain and evil to highlight our need for him, and to call us back to his goodness.

WHAT WE CAN LEARN FROM GOD'S PROMISE

God's promise to seed the seed of the woman reveals his plan to put down the rebellion, redeem humankind, and restore the four types of broken relationships.

The first part of Genesis 3:15 says, "I will put enmity between you [Satan] and the woman." Enmity means conflict, conflict between Satan and the woman, marked by extreme hostility. The second phrase, "and between your seed and her seed", signals the continuation of this conflict through the ages. More about this in Session 8.

The word "seed" in relation to the woman also points to one individual in particular. God says, "he [the seed of the woman] shall bruise your head, and you [the rival spirit] shall bruise his heel."

Several translations use the word "offspring" rather than "seed." But the literal meaning of the word "offspring" is "seed", which seems rather strange. Everyone knows that "seed" belongs to men, not to women. So God's promise foreshadows a virgin birth, telling us this individual will not be born through the usual agency of a man. He will not have a human father.

So who is his father? The only possible answer is God. Therefore, he will possess both a human nature and the nature of God. And since God is his father, he also will be of royal descent.

TELLING THE STORY

In summary of these things, Gospel Stoy-arc™ messaging asserts three basic facts arising from God's promise to send the seed of the woman into the world:

- The seed of the woman will be born of a virgin

- God will be his father, and therefore,

- The seed of the woman will have two natures: the nature of both God and man

Some people object to our asserting these facts; arguing that Genesis 3:15 does not use the words "virgin-born." And they're right. This understanding of God's promise in Genesis 3:15 is based on our knowledge of the rest of the story. We are able to the connect dots. Our messaging reflects a decision to share this now. Our goal is to enhance a lost person's understanding of who Jesus is.

As we tell Jesus' story, we're not limited to how it unfolds in history. How much did Adam and others know? The answer is likely not everything; but more than the Scriptures say. Consider Enoch, for example. In the genealogy of Genesis 5, it says that Enoch disappeared from the earth, "because God took him." That's all it says. But in the New Testament book of Jude, verses 14 and 15, we learn that Enoch prophesied:

> "Behold, the Lord comes with ten thousands of his holy ones, to execute judgment on all and to convict all the ungodly of all their deeds of ungodliness that they have committed in such an ungodly way, and of all the harsh things that ungodly sinners have spoken against him."

Enoch spoke of the Second Coming of Jesus! Yet Genesis 5 does not mention it; for a good reason, no doubt. But that was then. Holding back now doesn't make sense. There's even biblical precedent for doing the opposite; for using new knowledge to share meaning that wasn't understood at the time. In chapter 2 of his gospel, John recalled what Jesus said as he threw the money changers out of the Temple,

> "Destroy this temple, and in three days I will raise it up."

John and the other disciples didn't understand what Jesus meant until later, after he rose from the dead. John shared the meaning anyway. His stated intention was to recall signs that show Jesus is the Christ, the Son of God. Holding back would have stripped the event of its power to reveal Jesus' identity. We use the same principle as we tell Jesus' story.

Lesson 7

The hostility between...

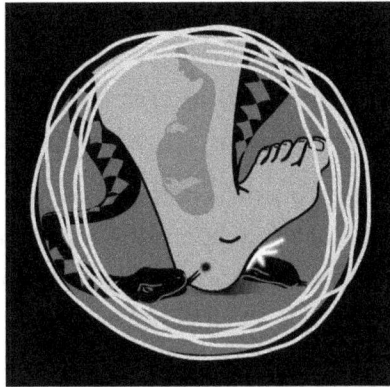

PRACTICE AND MEMORIZE — PANEL 5

The hostility between the serpent and "the seed of the woman" divided humanity into two sides going forward—the side of the serpent vs. the side of "the seed of the woman."

God's promise indicated there would be an epic conflict someday between the serpent and "the seed of the woman." God said that the serpent will "bruise" the heel of "the seed of the woman," causing him to experience pain and suffering. But God also said that "the seed of the woman" will "crush" the head of the serpent, indicating that "the seed of the woman" will win the epic conflict. (When you crush the head of a serpent, the serpent loses!)

The victory of "the seed of the woman" indicates that he is also a Savior. He will rescue people on the side of the serpent and restore all things, including the four types of broken relationships. Meanwhile, the serpent will do everything he can to deny the seed of the woman space in the world.

At the end of God's promise, one question remained: Who is "the seed of the woman?"

GOING DEEPER

The previous session introduced the promise God made in Genesis 3:15:

> "And I will put enmity between you and the woman, and between your seed and her seed. He shall bruise your head, and you shall bruise his heel."

The first phrase in this verse signals the start of an epic conflict. The second indicates that others join the war and identify with one of the sides. The third phrase indicates the conflict will end in an epic battle. It also uses "the seed of the woman" to designate a single person; and that he emerges the victor.

The hostility between the two sides is real, as they reflect the character and works of their leader. The side of the serpent reflects the brokenness of the four perfect relationships. It traffics in sin and death; and rebellion against God. Shame, hatred, and relational strife are its companions; pain and suffering are its fruit; the spread of unbelief is its mission. Not so, the side of the woman and her seed. They live by faith in the Savior. They show submission to him and God the Father. They reflect the goodness of restoration, righteousness, and life; integrity, love, and relational harmony. They experience blessing and victory over pain, suffering, and death. They spread their faith in the Lord and all that is good.

AN ONGOING CONFLICT

God's promise indicates the two sides will remain in conflict for the rest of human history. It continues to this day, the longest war ever. The serpent still seeks to spread the pain, suffering, and death, the sin, evil, and unbelief associated with its side. His goal is to spoil God's promise and deny space to the Savior and his seed.

The consequences of living on the serpent's side remain devastating; even for those living "the good life." They are actually more dead than alive. Others feel the brokenness and lostness of their plight. They feel stressed and harassed, and hated by others. Often they hate in return and are unable to forgive. They feel condemned by God and fear death and eternity. They live without purpose and hope.

Thankfully, it's still possible to change sides. Jesus is the seed of the woman. Through faith alone in him, you can experience the only true solution to the sentence of death. You can enjoy the peace and hope of eternal salvation. The restoration of relationships can be yours. This is why we're so passionate about telling Jesus' story.

AN EPIC BATTLE

The last phrase of the promise, "he [the seed of the woman] shall bruise your head, and you [the rival spirit] shall bruise his heel," points to an epic battle. In this battle, the seed of the woman suffers a heel bruise, indicating that the serpent will inflict pain and suffering on him, possibly unto death. However, the seed of the woman ultimately wins. He will "bruise" or crush the head of the serpent, signaling his defeat. Because when you crush the head of a serpent, it always dies.

So the seed of the woman will gain victory over the rival spirit. And by his victory, and through faith in him, he rescues people from the side of the serpent, redeeming them; and delivering them from the rival spirit's power and influence; and ultimately restoring them.

The rest of human history is the unfolding of God's plan to fulfill his promise to send the seed of the woman, the virgin-born savior, to defeat the rival spirit and restore all things. As the story unfolds, God reveals more. He reveals the family line of the Savior and more about his character, and the restoration he will bring. Meanwhile, the question remains, "Who is this person?"

Over time, God revealed more...

PRACTICE AND MEMORIZE — PANEL 6

Over many years, God revealed more about the character and family line of "the seed of the woman." He revealed that "the seed of the woman" would be a Savior and King. He would also be a Prophet and Priest.

God also revealed the circumstances of the Savior's birth, and of the miracles he would perform to prove his identity. Eventually, Jesus came into the world as the promised "seed of the woman." Jesus was born of a virgin as we would expect. He grew into adulthood and lived a perfect life. He also performed many miracles.

But the people of Jesus' day rejected him and murdered him on a cross. Jesus died willingly, knowing that his suffering and death were the "bruising of the heel" predicted in Genesis 3:15. Jesus also knew that his death would pay the penalty that people deserve for joining in the rebellion against God. Jesus spoke of his great love as motivation for dying to pay for our sin and rebellion, saying: "Greater love has no one than this, that someone lay down his life for his friends."

After three days, Jesus rose to new life in power and victory over sin and death. His resurrection marked the beginning of "the crushing of the serpent's head."

GOING DEEPER

Gospel Story-arc™ messaging refers in panel 6 to the rising action of Jesus' story in just a few words:

> Over time, God revealed more about the character and family line of "the offspring of the woman." He revealed that "the seed of the woman" would be a Savior and King. He would also be a Prophet and Priest.

Most of the messaging for this panel tells the story's climax; when Jesus comes into the world, lives a perfect life, performs miracles to prove his identity, dies on the cross, and rises again.

THE CLIMAX OF THE STORY

The Apostle Peter captured the sentiment of this part of Jesus' story in the sermon he preached on the Day of Pentecost. Acts 2:22-36 records what he said:

> Men of Israel, hear these words: Jesus of Nazareth, a man attested to you by God with mighty works and wonders and signs that God did through him in your midst, as you yourselves know—this Jesus, delivered up according to the definite plan and foreknowledge of God, you crucified and killed by the hands of lawless men.
>
> God raised him up, loosing the pangs of death, because it was not possible for him to be held by it. For David says concerning him, "I saw the Lord always before me, for he is at my right hand that I may not be shaken; therefore my heart was glad, and my tongue rejoiced; my flesh also will dwell in hope. For you will not abandon my soul to Hades, or let your Holy One see corruption. You have made known to me the paths of life; you will make me full of gladness with your presence."
>
> Brothers, I may say to you with confidence about the patriarch David that he both died and was buried, and his tomb is with us to this day. Being therefore a prophet, and knowing that God had sworn an oath to him that he would set one of his descendants on his throne, he foresaw and spoke about the resurrection of the Christ, that he was not abandoned to Hades, nor did his flesh see

corruption. This Jesus God raised up, and of that we all are witnesses.

Being therefore exalted at the right hand of God, and having received from the Father the promise of the Holy Spirit, he poured out this that you yourselves are seeing and hearing. For David did not ascend into the heavens, but he himself says, "The Lord said to my Lord, 'Sit at my right hand, until I make your enemies your footstool.'"

Let all the house of Israel therefore know for certain that God has made him both Lord and Christ, this Jesus whom you crucified.

In these words, Peter says that God accredited Jesus with signs, miracles, and wonders. After this, God delivered Jesus into the hands of lawless men who murdered him. Then God raised Jesus from the dead and exalted him as both Lord and Christ.

OUR MESSAGING

Gospel Story-arc™ messaging follows the flow of Peter's presentation. First, we call attention to the large amount of information about God and the seed of the woman revealed in the part of the story between Genesis 3:15 and the New Testament:

Over time, God revealed more about the character and family line of "the offspring of the woman." He revealed that "the seed of the woman" would be a Savior and King. He would also be a Prophet and Priest.

GOD ACCREDITED JESUS

Next, we say that God accredited Jesus through signs, miracles, and wonders; including the miracle of the virgin birth:

God also told of the circumstances of the Savior's birth, and of the miracles he would perform to prove his identity. Eventually, Jesus came into the world as the promised "seed of the woman." Jesus was born of a virgin at Christmas. He grew into adulthood and lived a perfect life. He also performed many miracles.

Throughout his time on earth, Jesus repeatedly claimed to represent and speak for God the Father. He declared himself the Christ and Savior of the world. The many miracles he performed accredited his claims.

LAWLESS MEN KILLED JESUS

The miracles should have convinced everyone. Jesus' murderers rejected the proof. They reacted to Jesus as loyal members of the serpent's side; aligned with evil in their unbelief. As Peter says, they were "lawless men" who "killed" Jesus. Thus, our messaging says:

> But the people of Jesus' day rejected him and murdered him on a cross.

Though Jesus' death was murder, our messaging emphasizes it was part of God's larger plan; and that Jesus, out of love, freely offered himself in sacrifice:

> Jesus died willingly, knowing that his suffering and death were the "bruising of the heel" predicted in Genesis 3:15. Jesus also knew that his death would pay the penalty that people deserve for joining in the rebellion against God. Jesus spoke of his great love as motivation for dying to pay for our sin and rebellion, saying: "Greater love has no one than this, that someone lay down his life for his friends."

GOD RAISED UP JESUS

Next, Peter asserts that God raised Jesus from the dead. He connects this amazing miracle to detailed Old Testament prophecies. Gospel Story-arc™ messaging does the same; but in reference to the prophecy of Genesis 3:15:

> After three days, Jesus rose to new life in power and victory over sin and death. His resurrection marked the beginning of "the crushing of the serpent's head."

GOD EXALTED JESUS

Peter closes his gospel presentation by calling attention to God's exalting Jesus at his right hand as both Lord and Christ. Gospel Story-arc™ messaging makes the same point as in connection with the first part of Panel 7, which comes next.

Forty days later...

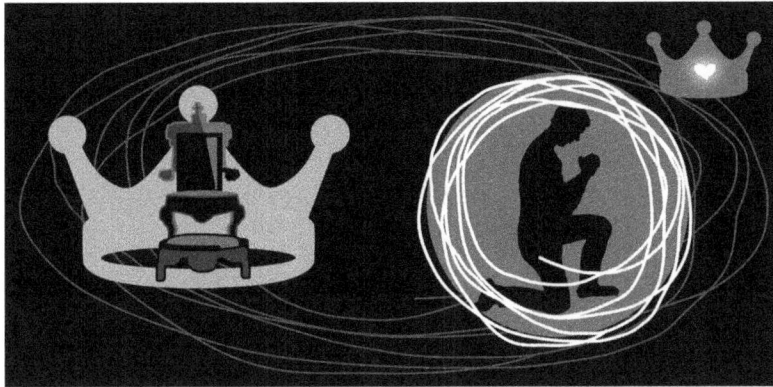

PRACTICE AND MEMORIZE — PANEL 7

Forty days later, Jesus ascended into heaven and sat down at the right hand of God to be exalted as King of kings and Lord of lords.

Jesus remains seated for now at the right hand of God the Father, where he is interceding for us as our high priest, and building his Church, calling people from every nation to believe in him.

Someday, Jesus will return to judge the earth for its sin and unbelief. Then, "every knee will bow and every tongue will confess that Jesus is Lord;" in other words, that he is the Savior and Restorer God promised to send. But it will be too late for people who refused to believe in Jesus in this life. They will be punished and separated from God forever.

Now, it's still possible for people to be saved from sin, brokenness, and judgment through faith in Jesus. Jesus said: "For God so loved the world, that he gave his only Son, that whoever believes in him should not perish but have eternal life."

Through faith in Jesus, Christians are forgiven and begin to experience restoration of the four broken relationships; although only in part for now. The restoration will be completed after the final judgment. Then, Jesus will deliver his kingdom to God the Father; and make all things new in the new heaven and new earth under God's rule.

GOING DEEPER

Jesus' ascension into heaven marked the beginning of his exaltation as "Lord of lords" and "King of kings"; while also providing strong proof of his identity as "the seed of the woman." With this in mind, the Apostle Paul linked confessing that "Jesus is Lord" to believing in our hearts that "God raised him from the dead":

> "If you confess with your mouth that Jesus is Lord and believe in your heart that God raised him from the dead, you will be saved."

Jesus' resurrection showed his amazing power over death as "the seed of the woman." And over the serpent; that he would finish crushing the head of the serpent someday when he returns. These are reasons why we should always include Jesus' resurrection in our gospel presentations.

Similar connections to Jesus' identity as "Lord" are found in the early Christian hymn Paul included in Philippians 2:5-11:

> "Have this mind among yourselves, which is yours in Christ Jesus, who though he was in the form of God, did not count equality with God a thing to be grasped, but made himself nothing, taking the form of a servant, being born in the likeness of men. And being found in human form, he humbled himself by becoming obedient to the point of death, even death on a cross. Therefore, God has highly exalted him and bestowed on him the name that is above every name, so that at the name of Jesus every knee should bow, in heaven and on earth and under the earth, and every tongue confess that Jesus Christ is Lord, to the glory of God the Father."

JESUS' RETURN

Jesus' story in Scripture does not end with Jesus' ascension and exaltation as Lord. It ends with the total restoration of all things. This includes the four types of perfect relationships that were broken in the rebellion near the beginning. Someday Jesus will return and complete the good work of salvation that he began. Revelation 21:1-8 summarizes what happens:

> "Then I saw a new heaven and a new earth, for the first heaven and the first earth had passed away, and the sea was no more. And I saw the holy city, new Jerusalem, coming down out of heaven from

God, prepared as a bride adorned for her husband. And I heard a loud voice from the throne saying, 'Behold, the dwelling place of God is with man. He will dwell with them, and they will be his people, and God himself will be with them as their God. He will wipe away every tear from their eyes, and death shall be no more, neither shall there be mourning, nor crying, nor pain anymore, for the former things have passed away.' And he who was seated on the throne said, 'Behold, I am making all things new.' Also he said, 'Write this down, for these words are trustworthy and true.' And he said to me, 'It is done! I am the Alpha and the Omega, the beginning and the end. To the thirsty I will give from the spring of the water of life without payment. The one who conquers will have this heritage, and I will be his God and he will be my son. But as for the cowardly, the faithless, the detestable, as for murderers, the sexually immoral, sorcerers, idolaters, and all liars, their portion will be in the lake that burns with fire and sulfur, which is the second death.'"

Much of the language used in Revelation 21:1-8 comes straight from the Old Testament book of Isaiah. For example, In Isaiah 65:17, the Lord spoke through the prophet, saying:

"For behold, I create new heavens and a new earth, and the former things shall not be remembered or come into mind."

OTHER CONNECTIONS

Here is a chart showing a sample of other connections between Isaiah and Revelation 21:1-8:

Revelation 21:1-8	Isaiah
21:1 – Then I saw a new heaven and a new earth, for the first heaven and the first earth had passed away, and the sea was no more."	65:17 – For behold, I create new heavens and a new earth, and the former things shall not be remembered or come into mind.

Revelation 21:1-8	Isaiah
21:3 – And I heard a loud voice from the throne saying, "Behold, the dwelling place of God is with man. He will dwell with them, and they will be his people."	25:9 – It will be said on that day, "Behold this is our God; we have waited for him, that he might save us. This is the Lord, we have waited for him; let us be glad and rejoice in his salvation."
21:4 – He will wipe away every tear from heir eyes, and death shall be no more, neither shall there be mourning, nor crying, nor pain anymore, for the former things have passed away.	25:8 – He will swallow up death forever; and the Lord God will wipe away tears from all faces, and the reproach of his people he will take away from all the earth.
21:5-6a – And he who was seated on the throne said, "Behold, I am making all things new." Also he said, "Write this down, for these words are trustworthy and true." And he said to me, "It is done! I am the Alpha and the Omega, the beginning and the end."	48:12 – "Listen to me, O Jacob, and Israel, whom I called! I am he; I am the first, and I am the last." 46:9-10 – "Remember the former things of old; for I am God, and there is no other, I am God, and there is none like me, declaring the end from the beginning and from ancient times things not yet done, saying, 'My counsel shall stand, and I will accomplish all my purpose.'"

Revelation 21:1-8	Isaiah
21:6b – To the thirsty I will give from the spring of the water of life without payment	55:1a – "Come, everyone who thirsts, come to the waters ..." 49:10 – They shall not hunger or thirst, neither scorching wind nor sun shall strike them, for he who has pity on them will lead them, and by springs of water will guide them. 66:12 – For thus says the Lord: "Behold, I will extend peace to her [Jerusalem] like a river, and the glory of the nations like an overflowing stream..."
21:7 – The one who conquers will have this heritage, and I will be his God and he will be my son.	43:4-7 – "Because you are precious in my eyes, and honored, and I love you, I give men in return for you, peoples in exchange for your life. Fear not, for I am with you; I will bring your offspring from the east, and from the west I will gather you. I will say to the north, Give up; and to the south, Do not withhold; bring my sons from afar and my daughters from the end of the earth, everyone who is called by my name, whom I created for my glory, whom I formed and made."

Revelation 21:1-8	Isaiah
21:8 – But as for the cowardly, the faithless, the detestable, as for murderers, the sexually immoral, sorcerers, idolaters, and all liars, their portion will be in the lake that burns with fire and sulfur, which is the second death."	30:33 – For a burning place has long been prepared; indeed, for the king it is made ready, its pyre made deep and wide, with fire and wood in abundance, the breath of the Lord, like a stream of sulfur, kindles it.

Other verses from Revelation and Isaiah could be added to show connections between what the two says about the coming total restoration of all things.

FINAL RESTORATION OF THE FOUR RELATIONSHIPS

Revelation 21:1-8 also describes God's restoration of the four types of relationships:

1) Revelation 21:3 and 7 refer to the restoration of broken relationships with God.

21:3 - "And I heard a loud voice from the throne saying, 'Behold, the dwelling place of God is with man. He will dwell with them, and they will be his people.'"

21:7 - "The one who conquers will have this heritage, and I will be his God and he will be my son."

These verses track with our earlier descriptions of a perfect relationship with God as a relationship marked by "not having any sin in your life; of always believing in God; always trusting in him; always doing his will; always being glad to see him; and always having him as a close friend."

2) Revelation 21:8 refers to the restoration of broken relationships with others:

21:8 - "But as for the cowardly, the faithless, the detestable, as for murderers, the sexually immoral, sorcerers, idolaters, and all liars, their portion will be in the lake that burns with fire and sulfur, which is the second death."

This verse describes the end of relationship dysfunctions, which tracks with our earlier descriptions of perfect relationships with others as "never getting into any arguments or fights with anyone, always living in perfect harmony with everyone, always loving them, and vice versa."

3) Revelation 21:4 and 21:6b hint at restoration of broken relationships with self:

21:4 - "He will wipe away every tear from their eyes, and death shall be no more, neither shall there be mourning, nor crying, nor pain anymore, for the former things have passed away."

21:6b - "To the thirsty I will give from the spring of the water of life without payment."

At least some of the mourning, crying, pain, and death referenced in these verses is tied to the fear and guilt and shame associated with a broken relationship with self. The conditions described are consistent with our being restored.

4) Revelation 21:1 refers to the restoration of relationships with everything in creation:

21:1 - "Then I saw a new heaven and a new earth, for the first heaven and the first earth had passed away, and the sea was no more."

21:5 - "And he who was seated on the throne said, 'Behold, I am making all things new.'"

These verses track with our earlier descriptions of what it would be like to enjoy a perfect relationship with creation; a world remade to be "completely safe and never dangerous; full of good only and never evil; full of resources to discover; with no obstacles hindering your ability to be manage those resources for good and for God's glory."

JUDGMENT AND FORGIVENESS

The messaging for Panel 7 explains there a time of final judgment is coming:

> Someday, Jesus will return to judge the earth for its sin and unbelief. Then, "every knee will bow and every tongue will confess that Jesus is Lord;" in other words, that he is the Savior and Restorer God promised to send. But it will be too late for people who refused to believe in Jesus in this life. They will be punished and separated from God forever..

But the messaging also emphasizes the hopeful possibility of God's forgiveness, through Jesus, his Son, whom he sent because of his great love for us:

> Now, it is still possible for people to be saved from sin, brokenness, and judgment through faith in Jesus. Jesus said: "For God so loved the world, that he gave his only Son, that whoever believes in him should not perish but have eternal life."

Through faith in Jesus, Christians are forgiven and restored to a relationship with God. They love God and desire to serve him. When Jesus comes, he will complete the restoration of all relationships. Prior to this will be final judgment. Meanwhile, Jesus gives grace to help in all our relationships. When he delivers his kingdom to God the Father, everything begins anew in the new heaven and new earth under God's rule.

Lesson 10

An Invitation to Believe

PRACTICE AND MEMORIZE

Are you ready to believe in Jesus?

If the answer is "Yes," then I've got some very good news! God's love for you is real and so is his promise to give eternal life to everyone who believes in Jesus. What Jesus said is true: "For God so loved the world, that he gave his only Son, that whoever believes in him should not perish but have eternal life."

It's important to know that a decision to believe in Jesus begins in your heart. Another Scripture verse puts it this way: "If you confess with your mouth that Jesus is Lord and believe in your heart that God raised him from the dead, you will be saved."

"Saved" means saved from judgment and rescued from the side of the serpent. The title "Lord" stands for everything we know about Jesus and his story, including his identity as "the offspring of the woman," the Son of God, and the Savior who died to pay for our sins. Believing in your heart that God raised Jesus from the dead means just that. Jesus' resurrection is singled out, because of its importance to his story. Without it, Jesus' story falls apart and faith becomes useless.

So what is your heart telling you to say about Jesus? If you have decided to believe in Jesus; say so. Celebrate your faith in Jesus with a friend, a relative, or the person who told you Jesus' story. Express gratitude to God in prayer for his forgiveness and the gift of eternal life. Tell Jesus himself what he now means to you by faith. Then go and tell others. They also need rescue from the side of the serpent through faith in Jesus; salvation from judgment as they believe in him.

GOING DEEPER

The New Testament contains several calls to believe, but all of them prioritize believing in who Jesus is. Too many Western formulations of the gospel skip who Jesus is for the sake of getting as quickly as they can to what Jesus did. This has the effect of subordinating propositions tied to Jesus' identity beneath those that tell what he did—in other words, prioritizing WHAT over WHO.

Please don't speed read this section.

The Scriptures themselves do just the opposite, not just in the New Testament, but throughout. As for the New Testament in particular, propositions about who Jesus is rise to the very top, as any objective analysis of New Testament gospel messaging will show. Not that New Testament writers never explain what Jesus did, or never argue for people to believe in the theological significance of what Jesus did. They do (and I love these explanations). But in gospel presentations to unbelievers, **who Jesus is comes first**. I will illustrate now from the writings of John and Paul, and from Jesus himself.

THE APOSTLE JOHN

In John 20:31 (ESV), the Apostle John writes:

> "... these [signs] are written so that you may believe that Jesus is the Christ, the Son of God, and that by believing you may have life in his name."

These words prioritize believing who Jesus is—he is the Christ, the Son of God.

Keep in mind, John wrote his gospel over 50 years after Jesus' resurrection. So he had a lot of time to think about how to craft his call to believe. He could have crafted it as more of a call to believe the abstract theology of what Jesus did. Please understand, I mean nothing disparaging by the word abstract. I'm referring to the conceptual thinking and logic that are central to theological argument.

John's call to believe in Jesus does not exclude any emphasis at all on Jesus' death for us. To the contrary, one of the many other titles John uses for Jesus early in his gospel is the Lamb of God, who takes away the sin of the world (1:29). This title obviously lays a foundation for the proposition that Jesus died for you. Besides this, John makes many other references to Jesus' death. So the point is not that John excludes from his writing any propositions about what Jesus did. It's that he organizes his call to action around propositions of who Jesus is, which are the types of propositions he also opens with in 1:1-14.

It's also worth noting that John calls for people to believe using only two of the many titles that belong to Jesus: Christ and Son of God. Leading up to 20:30-

31, John features numerous other titles that also belong to Jesus: Word, Lamb of God, King of Israel, King of the Jews, Son of Man, the Prophet, I AM, the Bread of Life, the Light of the world, the Good Shepherd, the Resurrection and the Life, the Way, the Truth, and the Life, the True Vine, Lord, and God. John's leaving these titles out of his call to action at the end doesn't make believing them optional. All of them point to truths about Jesus that everyone should embrace by faith. Nevertheless, John chose only the two, Christ and Son of God, to stand for all the others.

Finally, notice that John's call to believe doesn't come at the end of his gospel; it comes one chapter earlier, at the end of chapter 20. One reason could be because of the scene between Jesus and Thomas that precedes it. In 20:28, Thomas comes to the point of confessing with his mouth who Jesus is: Thomas answered him, "My Lord and my God." By inserting his call to believe immediately after this scene, John emphasizes the importance of someone expressing verbally what they believe about Jesus.

PAUL

The Apostle Paul gives similar emphasis in the call to believe that he lays out in Romans 10:9 (ESV):

> "If you confess with your mouth that Jesus is Lord and believe in your heart that God raised him from the dead, you will be saved."

Like John, Paul chooses only one of Jesus' titles to stand for the rest of what we know about him: the title Lord. Paul's use of this title should not be confused with so-called "Lordship salvation." Paul is not asking people to make Jesus their Lord with the intention of their sanctification becoming the means of their salvation. He is asserting that Jesus is Lord in accord with everything else Jesus' story reveals about him. So confessing with your mouth that Jesus is Lord simply means agreeing by faith with who Jesus is.

Paul's emphasis on believing in your heart recalls Jesus' teaching on the role our hearts play in relation to everything we think, say, and do, including making professions of faith. Our hearts are like control centers that command the resources under their authority to do their will. Psalm 27:8 illustrates how this works when a call to seek the Lord meets a heart of faith and obedience:

> You have said, "Seek my face."

My heart says to you, "Your face, O Lord, do I seek."

The heart of anyone who truly believes that God raised Jesus from the dead reacts similarly. It will rally its resources to believe and confess.

Elsewhere, Paul wrote that every true confession of faith in Jesus indicates the presence and power of God's Spirit. In 1 Corinthians 12:3 he said:

"No one can say 'Jesus is Lord' except in the Holy Spirit."

In the same verse, Paul also writes:

"No one speaking in the Spirit of God ever says, 'Jesus is accursed!'"

Paul's mention of believing in your heart that God raised Jesus from the dead focuses attention on what Jesus did. But once again, notice the order—first who Jesus is, then what Jesus did.

Just as the title Lord stands for everything we know about Jesus, so the resurrection stands for all that Jesus did and will do on into the future. Paul singles out the resurrection because it occupies such a strategic position in Jesus' story, like a keystone at the summit of an arch. It also supports Jesus being identified as the Christ.

Early on, people thought that Jesus' dying was an argument against his being the Christ. According to John 12:34, a crowd of people said as much when they responded to Jesus' prediction that he would be lifted up from the earth. The people perceived rightly that Jesus was indicating the manner of his death. He was going to die by crucifixion. So the people objected:

"We have heard from the Law that the Christ remains forever. How can you say that the Son of Man must be lifted up? Who is this Son of Man?"

The early church must have encountered this objection again and again as word of Jesus' death and resurrection spread from Pentecost. They forged an answer into what we now call a creed and circulated it widely. It was a creed that functioned as an apologetic in defense of the proposition that Jesus is the Christ. Yes, Jesus did die. But that doesn't eliminate him as the Christ. He died for our sins, in accord with the Scriptures. In other words, that was God's plan all along. Besides that, he didn't stay dead. He rose on the third day, once again, in accord with the Scriptures. And just in case, someone might scoff at the resurrection with an assertion that he didn't really die, the creed included stating that Jesus was buried.

By now, you recognize the creed as one that Paul quoted in his letter to the church at Corinth:

> "For I delivered to you as of first importance what I also received: that Christ died for our sins in accordance with the Scriptures, that he was buried, that he was raised on the third day in accordance with the Scriptures." (1 Corinthians 15:3-4 (ESV))

These words would not have been something new to the Corinthians, as they read Paul's letter for the first time. Paul even wrote that he was reminding the Corinthians that he had delivered these words to them once before, presumably on his first visit to the city. Paul also wrote that the Corinthians received these words, just as Paul himself had received them, as words of first importance.

It's true that Paul also introduces these words to the Corinthians as the gospel. Here's what he writes:

> "Now I would remind you, brothers, of the gospel I preached to you, which you received, in which you stand, and by which you are being saved, if you hold fast to the word I preached to you—unless you believed in vain." (Italics mine)

These words have led many to suggest that Paul meant for the creed to form a definition of the gospel and thus the content that gospel messaging boils down to—that Christ died for our sins in accordance with the Scriptures, that he was buried, that he was raised on the third day in accordance with the Scriptures. But there's something they overlook: the creed Paul quoted assumes that the Christ is Jesus. This means that even the creed leads with who Jesus is, not with what Jesus did. It's the only way the creed could have become meaningful in the early church. The Scriptures in the creed are Old Testament Scriptures that speak of the significance of the death of the Christ, and of the fact of his resurrection. Those Scriptures remained true no matter who the Christ turned out to be. Their power in the early church was in their application to Jesus.

When Paul describes the creed as of first importance, he was not saying that it was the first thing he mentioned. Acts 18:5 tells us the message that Paul led with:

"When Silas and Timothy arrived from Macedonia, Paul was occupied with the word, testifying to the Jews that the Christ was Jesus."

So Paul himself evangelized using the order he spells out in his Romans 10:9-10 call to believe: first, who Jesus is, followed by what Jesus did.

JESUS

Jesus' own awareness of his identity as the Christ, the Son of God, can be seen at every turn throughout the gospels. Like John and Paul, Jesus also prioritizes people believing in who he is as foundational to their embrace of what he was going to do. One example of this comes from Jesus' interaction with the Pharisees in Matthew 12 after Jesus cast out a demon from a man who also was blind and mute. Jesus healed the man, "so that the man spoke and saw." Matthew 12:23 reports:

"And all the people were amazed, and said, 'Can this be the Son of David?'"

Matthew's telling of what happened focuses attention on people responding by faith to who Jesus is. And the stakes could not be higher. Earlier in the chapter, Matthew reports Jesus knew that the Pharisees had already "conspired against him, how to destroy him" (12:14-15). This prompted Jesus to order certain people he healed not to make him known. In 12:17-21, Matthew explains Jesus was intent on fulfilling Isaiah's prophecy of his proclamation of justice, and of his bringing hope to the Gentiles. The clear implication is that Jesus was unwilling in that moment to do something that might disrupt the plan, either by the Pharisees' murdering him before his hour had come or by the people rising up then and there to install him as king. But then Jesus cast out the demon and heals the man the demon had afflicted.

The response of the people to this sign was not lost on the Pharisees. Unwilling not to allow their assessment of who Jesus is to stand, the Pharisees moved in quickly and said,

"It is only by Beelzebub, the prince of demons, that this man casts out demons." (12:24)

It was the worst slander possible. The Pharisees were accusing Jesus of being in league with Satan. At the beginning of Jesus' ministry, Satan tried to tempt

Jesus into bowing down to him; which would have turned Jesus into the same sort of character that Revelation's beast out of the sea will be someday. But Jesus refused to join forces with the devil, saying:

> "Be gone, Satan! For it is written, 'You shall worship the Lord your God and him only shall you serve.'" (Matthew 4:10, ESV)

Back in Matthew 12, Jesus knew that if he allowed the Pharisees' slander to stand, he would appear to lack confidence in his identity as the Son of David. He was already refusing to cooperate with people who wanted to install him as king. If he failed to speak up, the people might never move beyond amazement to actual faith in him. And his story might never spread beyond the Jews to the rest of the world. On the other hand, engaging the evil-hearted Pharisees also meant playing a dangerous game. They might just murder him now and leave his mission incomplete.

As you know, Jesus speaks up and defend his identity as the Son of Man. It is a lengthy defense and worth studying in every detail. But for now, I want to call your attention to what Jesus said in 12:36-37:

> "I tell you, on the day of judgment people will give account for every careless word they speak, for by your words you will be justified, and by your words you will be condemned."

Many people speculate about exactly what Jesus meant by words that are careless. According to Strong's, the Greek word behind the translation literally means lazy, shunning the labor one ought to perform. This suggests that careless words are idle words, and that they remain idle despite their having opportunities to be gainfully employed. When this understanding of careless words is plugged into the rest of what Jesus said in his defense against the accusation of the Pharisees, the meaning becomes clear. People will give account someday for their words being too lazy to acknowledge who Jesus is. It's as though the words of confession are just sitting there, resisting their employment, shunning the labor they ought to perform.

And what is the source of this resistance? According to Jesus, the source is the treasure of evil found in the hearts of evil people. To be sure, the words the Pharisees spoke against Jesus were evil words. Jesus' point is that the Pharisees will give an account for these words, as will everyone who refuses to employ their words to acknowledge who Jesus is. It's an accounting that ends in condemnation. By contrast, the accounting for words that do not shun the labor they ought to perform ends differently. These good words rise from treasures of good in people's hearts, prompting them to confess who Jesus is, and leading to their being justified.

Apart from the Pharisees, the events of Matthew 12 also show that Jesus wasn't willing to settle for anyone thinking only about what he did, even when they weren't so obviously evil in their assessment. The people who saw Jesus cast out the demon and heal the man who was blind and mute were amazed by what he did. But in the end, that wasn't good enough. One reason why Jesus so publicly engaged the Pharisees was because he wanted everyone watching to understand what he did in the context of who he is, the Son of Man.

WHY THE CALL TO BELIEVE MATTERS

In the end, the calls to believe coming from Jesus, John, and Paul are conceptually identical to one another:

1. All three prioritize who Jesus is as foundational to propositions about what Jesus did.

2. All three emphasize the imperative of people expressing their belief in Jesus by confessing such from their heart.

3. All three tie faith in Jesus to the ministry of God's Spirit.

4. All three refer to the salvation that results: life in his name (John); saved (Paul); and justified (Jesus).

Making a priority of who Jesus is in no way diminishes what Jesus did. To the contrary, who Jesus is informs and magnifies the significance of what Jesus did. In Philippians 2:5-11, Paul quotes from another early church confession:

> "Have this mind among yourselves, which is yours in Christ Jesus, who, though he was in the form of God, did not count equality with God a thing to be grasped, but made himself nothing, taking the form of a servant, being born in the likeness of men. And being found in human form, he humbled himself by becoming obedient to the point of death, even death on a cross. Therefore God has highly exalted him and bestowed on him the name that is above every name, so that at the name of Jesus every knee should bow, in heaven and on earth and under the earth, and every tongue confess that Jesus Christ is Lord, to the glory of God the Father."

My purpose in calling your attention to this hymn is simply to point out that everything in the hymn describing what Jesus did is bounded by who Jesus is. The hymn declares what Jesus did using seven verbs:

Did not count equality with God a thing to be grasped

Emptied himself (made himself nothing)

Took the form of a servant

Became (was born) in the likeness of men

Was found in human form

Humbled himself

Became obedient unto death, even death on a cross

Bracketing these are two declarations of who Jesus is—one at the beginning; the other at the end. The one at the beginning declares that, prior to his emptying himself and receiving the form of a servant, Jesus was in the form of God. Though scholars wrestle with the precise meaning of these words, the intent is clear: Jesus was no ordinary human being. Prior to emptying himself and taking the form of a servant, Jesus existed in full possession of the essential nature and character of God.* What follows in the hymn are the seven declarations of what Jesus did, with the first of these doubling down on who Jesus is (equal with God) as it makes its point. Once the list of seven is complete, the hymn declares that God the Father highly exalted Jesus, which ultimately prompts everyone to bend their knees and confess that Jesus Christ is Lord.

Keep in mind, Paul is exhorting believers to adopt the same mind as Jesus, the same humility and self-emptying, the same obedience and self-sacrifice, even if, like Jesus, it leads to our death too. So Paul is exhorting believers to do what Jesus did. But he embeds the exhortation in an understanding of who Jesus is. To Paul leading (and closing) with who Jesus is doesn't take away from the exhortation. It only enhances it and makes it more powerful, something that applies to gospel messaging that leads with who Jesus is.

CONSEQUENCES

In the end, asking people to believe what Jesus did before they believe who Jesus is ignores the plain teaching of Scripture. As expected, when we ignore the Scriptures, the consequences are undesirable. Among them is a tendency to disconnect from the larger story about Jesus told in Scripture.

Interlude

Megaphones and Funnels

You now have the full Gospel Story-arc® messaging in view. You've learned the seven movements, practiced the wording, and begun to see how the story holds together as a coherent whole. The next question is inevitable: **How do we use this in real life without reducing it to another quick formula?**

The material in this short but essential interlude clarifies the difference between **megaphone** evangelism and **funnel** evangelism. It explains why Gospel Story-arc™ messaging is designed to thrive in relational, multi-moment, story-first conversations—especially in a culture where many people lack the categories needed to understand a compressed gospel presentation. With this strategy in view, you'll be ready to step into Lessons 11–12 with clarity, confidence, and a realistic, hopeful approach to beginning gospel conversations.

The following material was adapted from "Story First: The Case for Come and See Evangelism" by Randal Gilmore...

One of my favorite Bible passages is Romans 10:13-15:

> "For 'everyone who calls on the name of the Lord will be saved.' How then will they call on him in whom they have not believed? And how are they to believe in him of whom they have never heard? And how are they to hear without someone preaching? And how are they to preach unless they are sent? As it is written, 'How beautiful are the feet of those who preach the good news!'"

The last two verses of this text contain a progression of communication events required to bring about the outcome stated in the first verse — "calling on the name of the Lord." Heralds of the good news must first be sent. Once sent, they must preach. The message they preach, the audience must hear and believe. Finally, the audience must call on the name of the Lord. Only then do they receive the promise of salvation declared at the beginning: "For 'everyone who calls on the name of the Lord will be saved.'"

The blueprint is God's, and I am totally committed to it. The rub comes in understanding exactly what it means to "preach" the good news. The original Bible word for "preaching" means to cry out or proclaim, conjuring up visions of someone making an announcement as a sort of town crier. It also refers to the work of an ambassador; someone charged with the near sacred duty of passing along an important message from a king. The underlying metaphors are not the same. Town-criers and ambassadors do not use the same style to share their messages. The latter will probably adopt a more soft-spoke and personal approach.

Town-crier style or not, "preaching" of any kind is a "communication event." When we break down what that means, we find both a message sender and receiver. We also find other elements common to most basic models of communication: feedback; message encoding; and message decoding (see Figure 1). "Preaching" takes in all of these through the various modes "preachers" use—verbal; written; audio; video; etc. "Preaching" also uses various rhetorical devices. And this is where, for the purposes of this book, things get interesting.

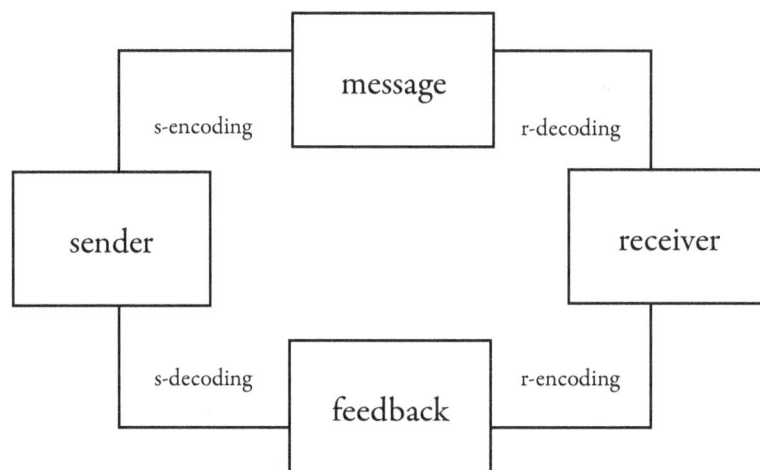

Figure 1 — Basic Model of Communication

MEGAPHONES

There are two additional metaphors we might use to describe the activity of "preaching." The first is a megaphone. The second is a funnel.

Certain properties of a megaphone make it a useful device. It can blast through background noise and gain the attention of an audience. It can make preaching more efficient; not slowed by two-way conversation. It stresses the type of conversation represented by the top half of the basic model; from senders to receivers without feedback.

In reality, feedback is always there in some fashion. It's just not what comes to mind when megaphones take the stage. Still, listeners on the receiving end of megaphone conversation do have their say. They move on when they tire of listening, which can happen in a short amount of time. Wise "preachers" understand this and the value of efficiency when crafting messages for megaphones. A single, efficiently crafted message works best.

In summary, there are four properties of megaphones, leading in turn to certain choices when using them to tell the good news. Megaphones (1) blast through background noise; (2) stress one-way, listener-targeted communication; (3) utilize single messages; and (4) require message efficiency.

FUNNELS

The second metaphor is a funnel. A funnel is the same as a megaphone; only with the mouth rotated to the bottom and the wider opening rotated to the top. This rotation makes a world of difference when it comes to sharing the gospel. Unlike megaphones, funnels take advantage of openings that already exist, even when the openings are small. In fact, they are designed to do this very thing; gain entry through small openings.

Funnels also give feedback more readily than megaphones. If you fill a funnel too quickly, it will overflow. The liquid rising toward the top of the funnel as you pour is feedback; telling you to slow down or stop altogether, to wait until the receptor is ready for more. Conversation funnels give similar feedback to message senders.

Picture a conversation funnel with its large opening on the sender side of the basic model. Its small opening points to the receiver side. Now think about the flow of conversation. A sender, in this instance, is able to fill the conversation funnel with more than one message; or with more than one kind of message. This represents listener-engagement and less dependence on message efficiency. Messages can be expanded instead and adjusted in response to feedback.

The contrast between conversation megaphones and funnels is complete:

- Megaphones can blast through background noise.
  Funnels take advantage of existing openings; even when they are small.

- Megaphones target listeners.
  Funnels engage listeners.

- Megaphones are for single messages.
  Funnels allow for more messages or more kinds of messages.

- Megaphones call for messages that are efficiently crafted.
  Funnels call for messages that can be expanded and adjusted to feedback.

IMPACT ON PRESENTING THE GOSPEL

The contrast between megaphones and funnels illustrates two models of gospel presentation found in Scripture. This often leads to a discussion of Peter's approach on the Day of Pentecost in Acts 2 versus Paul's approach on Mars Hill in Acts 17.

On the Day of Pentecost, Peter began by speaking directly about Jesus. His Jewish audience already understood God's promise of a Messiah, so he could start with the climax of the story. Paul, on the other hand, was addressing pagan Gentiles in Athens. On Mars Hill, he began with Creation itself—the starting point his audience most needed.

In reality, both presentations follow the same megaphone model; they simply begin at different points.

The "megaphone" approach blasts through background noise with a single, direct message. It's typically a one-way conversation, targeted at listeners, and carefully crafted for efficiency.

The second model—represented by funnels—works differently. Funnels take advantage of small openings for the good news. They allow for different starting points, emphasize two-way conversation, and unfold over multiple messages. This model leans toward message expansion rather than condensation.

We see this funnel model, for example, in the Gospel of John. While John offers many clear propositions about Jesus, he communicates primarily through narrative. In effect, his Gospel is a book-length gospel tract—and a book-length summary of the Gospel Story-arc. Its purpose is to foster belief that "Jesus is the Christ, the Son of God, and that by believing you may have life in His name" (John 20:30–31).

To accomplish this, John weaves in a sub-theme from the very first chapter: "Come and see." He uses these words twice in chapter 1—first from Jesus to two of John the Baptist's disciples (1:39), then from Philip to Nathanael (1:46). The woman at the well in John 4 uses a similar invitation to her neighbors (4:29). And here we find a fifth contrast between megaphones and funnels: megaphones say, "Listen to this!" while funnels invite, "Come and see."

Throughout this book, I will clarify the differences between megaphone and funnel approaches to gospel communication and make the case for Come and see evangelism. You may notice some overlap—certain aspects of megaphones can also be found in funnels—but each metaphor best illustrates a different way of engaging people with the good news.

I will also draw from my own experiences sharing the gospel in Japan. For many years, I have studied why the response to the gospel there has been so slow. Although Japan's spiritual climate is unique, I see growing similarities between what has happened there and what is now happening in other parts of the world, including North America.

For this reason, I invite you to begin "funneling" in your own re-tellings of the good news. Nothing would bring me greater joy than to see you and others take what I've written here and create new ways of sharing—so that countless people might call on the name of the Lord and be saved.

So let's begin. Come and see.

***

With this framework in mind, you can now see why Gospel Story-arc™ messaging is not simply a message to deliver, but a story to lead with—one that invites understanding, opens relational space, and creates natural next steps. The goal is not to abandon clarity or urgency, but to pair them with patience, listening, and wise pacing.

In the next two lessons, you'll learn practical ways to begin gospel conversations that align with this story-first approach. These tools will help you recognize openings, invite meaningful dialogue, and guide people into Jesus' story with confidence and compassion.

Lesson 11

How to Begin Gospel Conversations, Part 1

Has anyone ever told you the story behind who Jesus is?

In this lesson and the next, we'll practice using **testimonies** and **framing stories** as **conversation funnels** that naturally narrow toward the good news about Jesus.

Before we look at specific strategies, we need a clear definition. For our purposes, a **gospel conversation** is simply this:

> **Any conversation on an everyday topic that gradually narrows its focus to matters related to the gospel—who Jesus is, what He has done, who we are, and His call to believe and follow Him.**

You may begin by talking about work, family, a movie, a news story, or a personal struggle. As the conversation continues, you gently guide the focus toward the deeper issues the gospel speaks to—sin and brokenness, hope and forgiveness, identity and destiny, life and death.

A **conversation funnel** illustrates this movement:

- a wide opening at the top (ordinary topics),
- narrowing through stories and questions,
- leading toward Jesus and the gospel story at the bottom.

You'll see this picture in the graphics that follow. For now, keep the basic movement in mind: **from ordinary talk to deep gospel conversation.**

SIX PRINCIPLES THAT SHAPE OUR APPROACH

As we think about starting gospel conversations and guiding them through the funnel, six biblical and practical principles will shape our approach:

1. **Feelings of guilt, alienation from God, and shame** are part of the sen-

tence of death passed upon all descendants of Adam and Eve.

2. **Consequently, many people feel lost and broken**; stressed and harassed; hated by others; unable to forgive; condemned by God; without purpose, meaning, and hope for life and eternity.

3. **Lostness and brokenness in ANY of the four key relationships** (God, others, self, and creation) could be a lost person's greatest concern.

4. **Some lost and broken people don't feel lost or broken at all.**

5. **Faith in Jesus saves people** from all of their sin and brokenness.

6. **Evangelism is the beginning of discipleship** focused on appreciative love for Jesus. We're not just aiming for decisions; we're inviting people into a lifelong relationship of trust, discipleship, and joy.

These principles will guide the way we listen, the kinds of questions we ask, and the stories we choose to share. In the rest of this lesson, we'll see how they apply as we use personal salvation testimonies as conversation funnels. In the next lesson, we'll do the same with framing stories from Scripture and from everyday life.

WHY SOME PEOPLE DON'T FEEL THEIR BROKENNESS

When we say in the fourth principle that some lost and broken people "don't *feel* lost or broken," we're describing more than simple stubbornness.

Yes, some lost people may have **hearts of stone**. But others, in their sin, have simply fallen victim to a dynamic that affects all of us. The human brain has a limited number of "slots" for things we can pay attention to at any given time. When life feels overwhelming, people often push painful questions out of those active slots.

- Sometimes they put off thinking about their deepest needs.
- Sometimes they give up because they no longer believe there is any real solution for their pain.

Their minds shift to something else, and they trudge on—numb to their lostness and brokenness.

Still, no one is saved without, at some point, sensing their brokenness and sin, and their need for restoration. So the question becomes:

- How do we help them safely reactivate the pain and brokenness they've pushed into the background?

- How do we help them acknowledge the kind of brokenness that's most real to them—with God, with others, with self, or with creation?

The conversation funnel is one way God can use us to do this. It gives us a gentle, relational way to walk with people from ordinary talk into deeper realities their hearts have been trying to ignore.

GETTING STARTED

The fifth principle in the above list states:

Faith in Jesus saves people from all of their sin and brokenness.

Don't miss the word *all*. Many people treat "Jesus saves" as if it only means, "I go to heaven instead of hell when I die." That's why some gospel presentations begin with diagnostic questions like, "If you were to die tonight, do you know where you would spend eternity?"

A focus on heaven and hell is not wrong. But it is **not the only way** to draw our friends and loved ones into conversations about the Lord. Other pathways are available because of what we stated in the third principle:

Lostness and brokenness in any of the four relationships—with God, with others, with self, and with the rest of creation—may be a lost person's greatest concern.

This principle acknowledges that not everyone feels pain in their relationship with God.

- Some don't believe in God at all.
- Others do believe, but the pain they feel most is in their relationships with **others** (conflict, betrayal), with **self** (shame, anxiety, addiction), or with creation (loss, sickness, disaster, injustice).

A broken relationship with God is the **primary source** of all this pain. But in real conversations, we may need to **enter through one of the other kinds of brokenness first**—listening well there—before we can talk meaningfully about the deeper spiritual brokenness behind it.

FROM ORDINARY TALK TO DEEP GOSPEL CONVERSATION: THE CONVERSATION FUNNEL

If you're anything like me, you've struggled with how to draw non-Christian friends and relatives into **deep gospel conversations**.

I remember one evening when two Japanese men came to our home for English conversation. We talked about their families. We talked about their jobs. Then, out of nowhere, I tried to pivot into a full gospel presentation. It didn't work. Their faces went blank. They stopped talking. The room filled with awkward silence.

Since then, I've learned a great deal about how to invite people into deep gospel conversations—not in a way they resent or that puts them on the spot, but in a way that genuinely engages their hearts and encourages them to enter in. I call this approach **story-based gospel conversation**.

Barriers to deep gospel conversation exist by default. We know this. But not all types of barriers are the same.

- Some are **spiritual**, impossible to overcome without the Spirit of God.
- Others are **relational and cultural**, and these require wisdom and insight into how people see us and themselves.

If we ignore these and suddenly drop a deep gospel conversation into the middle of ordinary talk, we're likely to be confused and frustrated by the reaction.

That's what happened with my Japanese friends. We were enjoying everyday conversation about family and work. Then, with no bridge at all, I switched to a deep gospel presentation. For them, it felt like a sudden topic change from a distant "teacher," not an invitation from a close friend. So they shut down.

The first graphic (see below) shows what was happening.

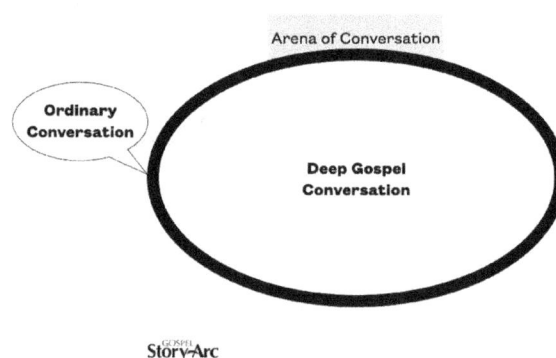

Arena of Conversation

Ordinary Conversation

Deep Gospel Conversation

Story-Arc

- On the **left**, we see ordinary conversation—like my talk with the men about families and jobs.

- On the **right**, we see **an Arena of Deep Gospel Conversation** surrounded by a thick black line.

The point is simple: ordinary conversation, by itself, cannot enter this arena. The thick line represents the relational and cultural barriers that block a sudden jump from small talk to gospel talk.

For a long time, I didn't see this clearly. It took repeated failures and a season of study before I finally realized I needed a different approach—one that honored how people naturally move from surface-level topics into deeper matters.

That's when I began studying the **science of story** and learning how to use a **story-based, story-first approach**.

The second graphic shows what needs to happen instead (see below).

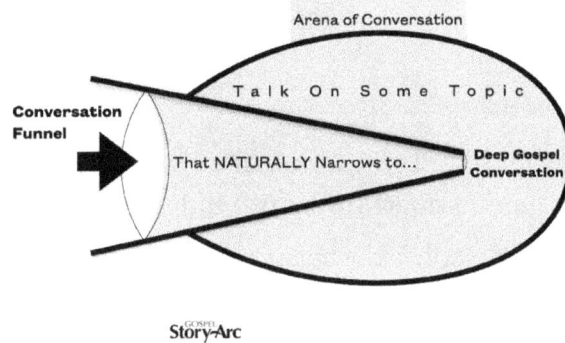

Story-Arc

Here, the talk that breaks into the arena of deep gospel conversation is shaped like a funnel:

- The **wide opening** at the top stands for the beginning of a conversation. We start with a broad topic of interest.

- As the conversation continues, it **narrows** toward gospel-related themes, guided by story and good questions.

- In time, we reach the bottom of the funnel, where Jesus and His story stand clearly in view.

Almost any subject can serve as a **starter topic**. One of the keys to success, however, is choosing a topic that truly grabs the other person's interest and then using a well-designed story to narrow the focus to gospel themes. Thoughtful questions then form part of an engaging journey as the funnel narrows. More about this in the next lesson, where I summarize four simple keys to effectiveness. For now, let's look at a concrete example of how this works using your salvation testimony.

YOUR SALVATION TESTIMONY: ONE KIND OF STORY THAT CREATES A DEEP GOSPEL CONVERSATION FUNNEL AND SURFACES FELT BROKENNESS

A **salvation testimony** is a personal story of your own experience. It's how you found the solution to sin and brokenness through faith in Jesus.

For example, you might ask for the privilege of sharing Gospel Story-arc® messaging by saying:

> "There was a time in my life when I felt **guilty** and **ashamed**. But then someone told me a story about Jesus that changed my life. Now I feel so **forgiven** and **loved** by God. Has anyone ever shared Jesus' story with you?"

Notice how this works:

- The first two boldfaced words describe awareness of sin and feelings of pain and brokenness apart from faith in Jesus.
- The second pair describes the change that came through hearing Jesus' story.
- Then you ask permission to share more.

This simple pattern helps form a **conversation funnel**:

- You start with your own experience of brokenness.
- You name the change Jesus brought.
- You invite the other person to hear His story, not just yours.

Try this with a partner. Here is a template you can use to fill in words from your own testimony:

There was a time in my life when I felt _____ and
_____.

But then someone told me a story about Jesus that changed my life.

Now I feel _____ and _____.

Has anyone ever told you the story behind who Jesus is?

The challenge with using your salvation testimony to surface someone else's hidden pain is that **your pain may not be their pain.** This underscores the importance of:

- asking questions at the beginning of your conversations,
- and using active listening to discern what their hidden pain might be.

Even then, you may still encounter a quiet reaction such as, "I guess that worked for you, but I don't think it will work for me. I'm not the religious type."

That's okay. Your salvation testimony is not a magic formula. It is simply one way to say, **"I found the solution to my deepest needs when I heard Jesus' story."** God can use that in ways you cannot see.

So it is always good to be ready—to have your salvation testimony prepared, to know how to ask permission, and to trust the Spirit of God with the results.

ASK FOR PERMISSION

One simple permission-giving way to begin a gospel conversation is to ask:

"Has anyone ever told you the story behind who Jesus is?"

This question is more neutral than, "If you died tonight..." yet it still opens the door to talk about Jesus. It doesn't assume the person feels guilty or afraid of death at that moment. Instead, it invites them to consider a story—Jesus' story—and gives you room to connect that story to the kind of brokenness they feel most, whether it's with:

- God,
- others,
- self,
- or the rest of creation.

In other words, this question can help **bring a buried concern back into one of those "attention slots"** in the mind, in a way that feels relational and respectful.

But what if they say,

"I'm not interested in religion"?

You might respond:

"Neither am I, when it comes to a lot of the religious stuff that's out there. But that's what I love about Jesus' story. Do you mind if I share it with you?"

If they still decline, you can simply say:

"No problem—maybe some other time."

Then you can consider one of the other strategies from this lesson or from the next conversation you have with them.

A second permission-giving way to begin is with this question:

"I've been learning how to tell the story of Jesus. **Would you mind if I practiced it now with you?**"

This approach is often helpful with friends and relatives you've already talked with about spiritual things. You can adjust this simple wording to fit many different situations. In every case, your first goal is the same:

Ask for permission to share Jesus' story.

How to Begin Gospel Conversations, Part 2

In the last lesson, you practiced using your testimony as a conversation funnel. In this lesson, we'll take the same idea and apply it to framing stories—stories from Scripture, from movies, from songs, and from everyday life that help people see their own brokenness and point toward Jesus.

Our goal is the same:

To move from ordinary talk into deep gospel conversation in a way that feels natural, respectful, and hopeful.

WHAT IS A FRAMING STORY?

For our purposes, a framing story is:

Any story you share (from Scripture, from a movie, from real life) that "frames" how someone sees their own brokenness and need, and then points toward Jesus and His story.

A framing story doesn't replace the gospel. It prepares the heart to hear the gospel by:

- surfacing the kinds of brokenness people already feel,
- naming the "rules of the world" they live under, and
- hinting at the possibility of a different way to live by faith in Jesus.

Stories are powerful because they bypass defenses. People who would argue with a sermon will often lean in to a story.

PARADIGMS: THE "RULES OF THE WORLD" INSIDE A STORY

Every story takes place in a "world" that runs by certain rules—what we might call paradigms:

- "This is how life works."

- "This is how people treat each other."

- "This is what you must do to survive."

Those rules may be right or wrong, good or evil, hopeful or hopeless. But they are always there.

When we use a framing story as a conversation funnel, we pay attention to:

- The rules of the story's world – What kind of world is this?

- The pain those rules create – Who gets hurt, and how?

- The change the story offers – What has to happen for things to be healed, set right, or made new?

Once we see those three things, we can gently help a friend compare the rules of the story world with the way Jesus describes reality in His story. That comparison (or paradigm juxtaposition) can open the door to deep gospel conversation.

AN EXAMPLE FROM SCRIPTURE

Consider the story of the Good Samaritan in Luke 10:25-37. The story begins with Jesus stating the paradigm that would be on display: "Love your neighbor as yourself."

Next, he tells the story of a man who fell among thieves on his way to Jericho and was left for dead. He tells how a priest and then a Levite saw him and pass him by. Then he tells of a Samaritan who stops, binds the man's wounds, and takes him to a place where he can recover.

So this story contains its own juxtaposition of paradigms: Carelessness for the lives of others vs. Love your neighbor as yourself (even when it costs you).

Conversation about these "rules" might begin with sharing a news story on "bullying." You might ask the lost person you're sharing with to react: "What do you think about bullying like this?"

As the conversation continues, you might say: "Bullying reminds me of the opposite of what Jesus taught in the story of the Good Samaritan." Review the gist of the story if needed.

Then say:

> "Jesus used the story of the Good Samaritan to teach, 'Love your neighbor as yourself.' Other times, he even said, 'Love your enemies.'"

Give the person you're sharing with a chance to weigh in. Then say:

> "I think bullying represents a totally different worldview than the one Jesus taught. It sounds more like "survival of the fittest" or "every person for himself.""

Then say:

> "Which do you prefer everyone would live by?"

Give the person you're sharing with a chance to answer. Then say:

> "How would something like 'love your neighbor as yourself' change your life? Your family? Your workplace?"

Give the person you're sharing with a chance to answer, of course. Then say:

> "Did you know that God promised at the beginning of history to solve problems like bullying and people living by 'every person for himself'? Would you like to hear more?"

The story of the Samaritan woman in John 4 is another example of a "third-party framing story." It tells about the woman's pain and brokenness prior to her encounter with Jesus. Other stories in Scripture also "frame" the change that takes place after someone meets Jesus. For example: Nicodemus; Andrew; Philip; Peter; Nathanael; Mary Magdalene; the woman who anointed Jesus' feet with perfume; the Ethiopian Eunuch; Simon the Magician; Cornelius; Lydia; the Philippian jailer; and numerous others.

AN EXAMPLE FROM A MOVE: I CAN ONLY IMAGINE

Let's look at one concrete example: the movie *I Can Only Imagine*.

The film tells the backstory of Bart Millard and the song he wrote. In the opening scenes, we watch Bart grow up in a world marked by superficial and broken relationships:

- He rakes leaves for his grandmother, alone—no friends, no real conversation about his work. He gets paid and rides away—still alone.

- His earphones become a symbol of isolation—he disappears into his own private world.

- His mother leaves him at camp.

- His girlfriend seems to fade from his life once camp ends.

- Most painfully, his father's anger and abuse destroy Bart's sense of safety, love, and belonging.

If we listen carefully, we can hear the "rules of the world" this story introduces:

- You are on your own.

- People leave.

- Fathers hurt you, not help you.

- If you mess up, it's your fault, and you should be ashamed.

Those rules add up to what you once called the "death of community"—a life beyond the pale, where someone is stuck on the outside looking in.

So what sets Bart free from this destiny?

In a word: **forgiveness**.

As Bart learns to forgive his father, the world begins to change:

- His relationship with his dad is restored.

- His relationship with God is renewed.

- His creativity, music, friendships, and calling come back to life.

Forgiveness opens the door back into community—not just with other people, but with God Himself. And this, of course, points beyond Bart's story to the larger story of Jesus:

> **Jesus forgives His enemies and restores broken people to community with God, with others, and with themselves. Then He calls us to forgive as we have been forgiven.**

This is what makes *I Can Only Imagine* a powerful framing story. It surfaces the pain of relational brokenness and the longing for restoration, then hints at the deeper power of forgiveness in Jesus.

SAMPLE CONVERSATION QUESTIONS USING I CAN ONLY IMAGINE

Here's how *I Can Only Imagine* can become a conversation funnel—starting wide, then narrowing toward Jesus.

You might begin with a simple starter:

"Have you ever seen the movie I Can Only Imagine?"

If they say yes, you could continue with questions like these (adjust and translate as needed):

1. Opening the Conversation (Wide End of the Funnel)

"Which character in the movie did you relate to most, and why?"

"How did you feel as you watched Bart becoming more and more isolated from people in his life?"

These questions stay close to the story, but they gently invite emotion, empathy, and self-reflection.

2. Surfacing Brokenness and the "Rules of the World"

Now you move a little deeper:

"Have you ever experienced a relationship that felt so broken it seemed like it could never be repaired? What happened?"

"If forgiveness had been possible in that situation, how might things have been different? How might forgiveness change things now?"

"Is there anyone in your life you struggle to forgive right now?"

"Some people say it's impossible to forgive an enemy. Do you agree or disagree?"

Notice what is happening here:

- You're not preaching.
- You're not forcing the conversation.
- You're asking questions that help the other person name their own pain and the "rules" they live by:

  "If someone hurts you deeply, the relationship is over."

  "To stay safe, you must cut people off."

  "I will never forgive ___."

This is exactly what a framing story is meant to do: bring buried pain into the light so it can be brought to Jesus.

3. Turning the Corner Toward Jesus

Once you've listened well and the person has shared something of their own experience, you can gently narrow the funnel toward the gospel:

"In the movie, what do you think helped Bart move toward forgiving his father?"

"How do you think his experience of God's forgiveness affected the way he saw his dad?"

"What do you think your life and relationships would look like if forgiveness really began to 'rule'—if forgiveness had the last word?"

Then you can ask questions that open the door directly to Jesus:

"What do you think of this idea: we are made for community—for deep, meaningful, loving relationships with others?"

"Has anyone ever shared with you what Jesus actually teaches about forgiveness?"

At this point, you can use the neutral question from the previous lesson:

"Has anyone ever told you the story behind who Jesus is?"

If they give permission, you now have a clear path:

- You've talked about a story of brokenness and forgiveness (I Can Only Imagine).
- You've surfaced their own experiences of relational pain.
- You've hinted that Jesus has something to say about all of this.

Now you can share Jesus' story (using Gospel Story-arc messaging) as the framing story that makes sense of all other stories.

FOUR KEYS TO EFFECTIVE FRAMING STORIES

There are four keys to the effective use of framing stories to funnel the way to deep gospel conversations. The graphic (see next page) illustrates the four keys at work in a conversation outreach called "The Mystery of the Orphan Tsunami and the Resurrection of Jesus Christ."

(This material is available from the Gospel Story-arc Project and can be adapted to a formal ESL class or to casual one-on-one conversation. It also works well translated into Japanese.)

Key 1: Subject matter that captures interest

First, I choose subject matter I know will interest my target audience. For Japanese listeners, the orphan tsunami is a natural choice. Tsunamis are part of everyday life in much of Japan. There is also strong interest in "religious" ques-

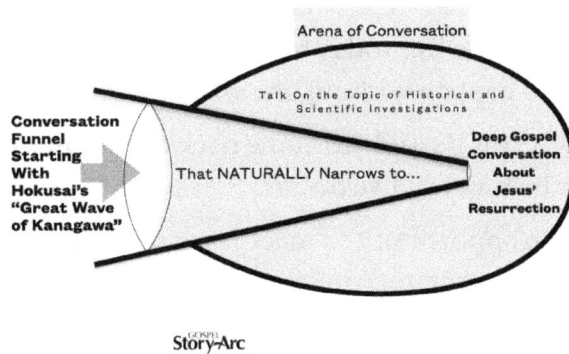

tions about life, death, and what comes after. If we can show that resurrection is possible, people will want to explore it.

Key 2: A starter topic that opens the door

Second, I use a starter topic to open the conversation. In this outreach, we begin by showing Hokusai's famous woodblock print, The Great Wave off Kanagawa. This image is a Japanese icon. It instantly engages the heart of a Japanese person.

I then ask simple questions about the print and how it is used in Japanese culture and around the world. These questions keep us in ordinary conversation while gently moving us toward something deeper.

Key 3: A featured story that narrows the focus

Next, I narrow the topic to the story of Japan's orphan tsunami of the year 1700. This is the featured story. I wrote it with a clear connection to Hokusai's print so the transition feels natural, not forced.

The story is crafted in two parts:

- Part 1 invites listeners into the **emotion and mystery** of the orphan tsunami—the fear of a giant wave that arrives without warning and the historical dilemma of not knowing when or where a future tsunami might strike.

- Part 2 shows the kinds of **tools scientists and historians** used to solve the mystery. This becomes a bridge: Christian historians use similar tools when investigating the resurrection of Jesus.

By the end of Part 2, listeners are already thinking about **evidence, history, and resurrection**, which leads naturally to a conversation about the mystery of Jesus' death and rising again.

Key 4: Conversation questions that invite the heart

Finally, I craft conversation questions from the story and related content. For example:

- "Have you ever had to evacuate your home because of a warning that something bad was about to happen? What happened?"

- "What would life be like today for people who live near the ocean if tsunamis could happen without any warning at all?"

- "If you knew it was possible to come back to life after you die, how would that change the way you live now?"

- "If you had the opportunity to meet Jesus and talk with Him, what would you say or what question would you ask?"

Some of these questions seem to have little to do with religion at first. Others are more obviously spiritual. The key is that **each question arises naturally from the material** and invites the other person to share:

- something that has happened to them,

- or something they think and feel about life, death, and meaning.

These questions help people open up. They also reveal personal values and worldview in a way that doesn't feel like a test.

OPTIONAL PRACTICE: USING AI TO HELP YOU DEVELOP CONVERSATION QUESTIONS

If you have access to an AI assistant (such as ChatGPT or a similar tool), you can use it as a practice partner to help you build conversation funnels around almost any story—movies, books, songs, news stories, or Bible passages.

AI is not a replacement for prayer, wisdom, or personal preparation. But it can help you:

- notice the "rules of the world" (paradigms) in a story,

- surface the kinds of brokenness the story reveals, and

- draft discussion questions that move naturally toward Jesus and the gospel.

Here is a sample prompt you can use or adapt:

AI Practice Prompt for Framing Stories

"I want to have deep gospel conversations using stories. Help me analyze the story [insert movie / book / song / Scripture passage] as a framing story.

1. Identify the main 'rules of the world' (paradigms) in this story—how life works, how people treat each other, and what someone must do to survive or succeed.

2. Show how those rules create brokenness in relationships with God, with

others, with self, or with creation.

3. Describe how Jesus' story offers a different set of rules and a path to healing and restoration.

4. Write 8–10 discussion questions that:

   • start with the story itself,

   • then move to someone's personal experience,

   • and then naturally open the door for me to ask, 'Has anyone ever told you the story behind who Jesus is?' so I can share Gospel Story-arc® messaging."

After you receive the AI's response, you can:

- Edit the questions into your own voice.

- Shorten the list to 5–6 questions you feel comfortable using.

- Practice asking and answering them with a partner in your training group.

The goal is not to depend on AI, but to use it as a tool to speed up your preparation so you can spend more time actually listening to people and sharing Jesus' story in real conversations.

WHY THE USE OF FRAMING STORIES FEELS NATURAL INSTEAD OF LIKE "BAIT-AND-SWITCH"

When we use subject matter people care about, a natural starter topic, a well-chosen story, and thoughtful questions, conversations feel less forced. We are not suddenly "switching topics" or springing a hidden agenda on someone.

Instead, we are walking with them through a story and genuinely asking what they think and feel. Along the way, we help them see the deeper issues the gospel addresses and invite them, when they are ready, into Jesus' story.

This is the heart of the **conversation funnel**:

- start wide,

- walk with them through a story,

- ask questions that invite the heart to respond,

- and gently narrow toward the good news of Jesus.

A SAMPLE FLOW OF CONVERSATION AROUND A FRAMING STORY

Tell a "framing story" that features a paradigm that puts either brokenness or restoration on display	Start the Conversation	Talk About How the Paradigm Impacts Them	Gospel Story-arc® Messaging
For example:	Ask:	Ask:	Ask:
An online news story about bullying	Have you heard about this?	What did you think?	Did you know the problem of _____ goes all the way back to the beginning of Jesus' story?
A popular movie or television show	Did you see this? OR	What do think the world would look like if everyone lived by that rule?	
A book	Have you ever read... [fill in the story or book title]? OR	How would your life would change if you always _____?	Would you like to hear more about it?
A viral video	Did you see...[fill in a video or movie title, or television show]? If "No", ask: Can I tell you about it?	How would it change your family? Your school? Or the place where you work?	Share Gospel Story-arc Messaging

Bonus 1

Evangelism Best Practices

BEST PRACTICE #1—DISCIPLESHIP (AND TRAINING)

"The two disciples heard him say this, and they followed Jesus."
John 1:37

"Him" in this verse is John the Baptist. "The two disciples" are Andrew and Philip. Before Andrew and Philip began to follow Jesus, they received training from John the Baptist. The wilderness-going forerunner taught them well. He discipled Andrew and Philip to recognize Jesus as the Christ, the Son of God, the Prophet, Priest, and King, sent in fulfillment of God's promises. In 1:27, John the Baptist humbly points others to look beyond his ministry as forerunner to "he who comes after me, the strap of whose sandal I am not worthy to untie." In 1:29 and 36, he declares Jesus "the Lamb of God" (previously, "the Lamb who takes away the sin of the world"; the second reference was likely a literary device used by John the Apostle to underscore the role of God's lamb as Conqueror—see Revelation 5:6-14; 6:1; 8:1; and 21-22, along with numerous other references to the victorious Lamb). In 1:30, John the Baptist indicated that Jesus ranked before him. In 1:32-33, he established the special link between Jesus and the Spirit of God, saying that he saw the Spirit of God descending on Jesus from heaven and remaining on Him. He finishes in 1:34: "And I have seen and have borne witness that this is the Son of God."

It's no wonder the hearts of Andrew and Philip turned quickly to faith in Jesus and then to sharing him as they did. John the Baptist trained them to understand the overarching story told in Scripture and to see in Jesus the fulfillment of its major themes and promises.

BEST PRACTICE #2—FOLLOW JESUS AND LEARN DIRECTLY FROM HIM

"The two disciples heard him say this, and they followed Jesus.
Jesus turned and saw them following and said to them, 'What
are you seeking?' And they said, 'Rabbi' (which means Teacher),
'where are you staying?' He said to them, 'Come and you will see.'
So they came and saw where he was staying, and they stayed with
him that day, for it was about the tenth hour."
John 1:37-39

Andrew and the others began following Jesus and learning from him directly. This overflowed into a constant stream of sharing their faith and experiences with others. Today we receive direct-from-Jesus training and direct-with-Jesus fellowship through the Word of God; through prayer; and through his ever-presence with us. We get to watch as Jesus works in our lives. Still, the written Word of God is primary; the touchstone for determining what is true. Applying God's Word, we must learn to recognize Jesus' presence whenever, wherever, and however He reveals Himself. This requires intention and constant awareness. It means taking to heart what we learn directly from Jesus, not for the sake of knowledge alone, but to govern the way we think, live, and interpret the world.

The evangelism best practice of following Jesus and learning directly from him turns our present-day invitations to "Come and See" into genuine, real-life opportunities for others to enter with us into a life of faith in Jesus.

BEST PRACTICE #3—TAKE INITIATIVE

"He first found his own brother Simon and said to him, 'We have
found the Messiah' (which means Christ)."
John 1:41

"Philip found Nathanael and said to him, 'We have found him
of whom Moses in the Law and also the prophets wrote, Jesus of
Nazareth, the son of Joseph.'"
John 1:45

Andrew and Philip took the initiative to share the good news about Jesus. They didn't wait for Simon and Nathanael to approach them. They knew it was their responsibility to make Jesus known before Simon and Nathanael asked. The same will hold true for most of our opportunities to share. Lost might come to us with questions about Jesus; but it's the exception, not the rule. In John 3, Nicodemus went to Jesus at night to escape the notice of his peers. He knew something was missing in his life, and he eventually overcame his hesitation about approaching Jesus; but only because he had cover. Most lost people will never approach us, no matter how much cover is available. Some don't even realize they are lost; or are too proud, distracted, or afraid to approach us. Waiting for them to come to us translates into their never hearing.

BEST PRACTICE #4—SHARE VERBALLY

"He first found his own brother Simon and said to him, 'We have found the Messiah' (which means Christ)."
John 1:41

"Philip found Nathanael and said to him, 'We have found him of whom Moses in the Law and also the prophets wrote, Jesus of Nazareth, the son of Joseph.'"
John 1:45

The fourth best practice stems from the same verses, giving rise to the third. Andrew and Philip both shared about Jesus verbally.

In recent years, there's been discussion about whether Christians should even try to share verbally with others. So-called experts say, "Share the gospel at all times, and, if necessary, use words." Some adopt this as their mindset and stop sharing altogether; no Gospel Story-arc summaries, stories, paradigms, or juxtapositions—no verbal sharing with unbelievers at all. We believe our lives must match what we say with our lips; but that doesn't mean "mum's the word!" Non-Christians do not figure out the gospel just by watching. Keep in mind the progression I brought up at the beginning of Chapter 2, the one we find in Romans 10:14-15:

"How then will they call on him in whom they have not believed? And how are they to believe in him of whom they have never heard? And how are they to hear without a preacher? And how are they to preach unless they are sent? As it is written, 'How beautiful are the feet of those who preach the good news!'"

BEST PRACTICE #5—IDENTIFY WITH OTHER CHRISTIANS

"He first found his own brother Simon and said to him, 'We have found the Messiah' (which means Christ)."
John 1:41

"Philip found Nathanael and said to him, 'We have found him of whom Moses in the Law and also the prophets wrote, Jesus of Nazareth, the son of Joseph.'"
John 1:45

Both Andrew and Philip referred in their witness to others who also had discovered the truth about Jesus: "we have found the Messiah, we have found him of whom Moses in the Law and also the prophets wrote." Notice they said "we". Christian community plays a vital role in fostering growth after someone becomes a believer. Growth is stifled in so many ways when a professing Christian remains detached. How to live as a Christian cannot be learned apart from community. Patience and forgiveness, for instance, cannot be practiced in isolation from others.

Witnessing for Christ is most often a "team effort." Few lost people become Christians through the influence of a single person. This is the idea behind Paul's words in 1 Corinthians 3:6: "I planted, Apollos watered, but God gave the increase."

BEST PRACTICE #6 — EMPHASIZE DISCOVERY AND FULFILLMENT

"He first found his own brother Simon and said to him, 'We have found the Messiah' (which means Christ)."
John 1:41

"Philip found Nathanael and said to him, 'We have found him of whom Moses in the Law and also the prophets wrote, Jesus of Nazareth, the son of Joseph.'"
John 1:45.

Lost people might wonder whether they will go to heaven when they die. Meanwhile, they also wonder:

- Is there any purpose in my life?
- Is there any grand plan for this world?
- Why do bad things happen to me?
- What can be done about my pain?
- What can be done about the heart-breaking loss I have experienced?
- How am I ever going to get ahead?
- What about the evil that's in the world?
- What about the evil in my own heart?
- How can I get a fresh start?
- How can I have a better marriage?
- What can I do about kids?
- How can I put my marriage or family back together?
- Where can I find true meaning and peace?

My life seems so empty. Nothing seems to work. Drugs, alcohol, sex, technology, sports, work, materialism, and consumerism—none of these fill my life with meaning and peace.

The Gospel Story-arc method emphasizes that Jesus came to forgive and give life to the full now (John 10:10); that God is at work now. This doesn't mean problems go away when someone becomes a believer. No, no, a thousand times no. In some cases, that's when the problems begin! I've known three people who were stricken with cancer and died within months of their becoming believers. We don't shut our eyes to the heavy burdens of a fallen, sin-cursed world. We emphasize instead that answers to life's problems are found in Christ; that through him we can embark on a fulfilling journey of discovery. We can endure and even thrive. Jesus often taught on the blessings of living under his rule now; of overcoming the world and the tribulations it brings. Evangelism best practices dictate that we share our own sense of personal discovery of these blessings, and of the fulfillment they bring to our lives.

BEST PRACTICE #7—USE THE SCRIPTURES

"...of whom Moses in the Law and also the prophets wrote."
John 1:45

Philip anchored his witness to Jesus in the Scriptures. He did not rely solely on his personal experience to share. Reasons why anyone should believe in Jesus come straight out of the Scriptures. They reveal who Jesus is and his role in God's plan for redeeming and restoring all things. The Scriptures also empower our witness. In 1 Peter 1:23, Peter wrote: "...you have been born again, not of perishable seed but of imperishable, through the living and abiding word of God." The new birth in Christ is a marvelous miracle that could never happen apart from God and his Word. When we use the Scriptures to share who Jesus is, we are tapping into divine power, far beyond on our own talents and abilities. This doesn't mean that our first job is to lay out everything we know about the Bible, or even to convince people that the Bible really is the Word of God. We don't even have to always give the reference to verses we quote. Hebrews 4:12 says: "For the word of God is living and active, sharper than any two-edged sword." Someone has observed. "You don't have to believe in a sword for a sword to be used against you."

BEST PRACTICE #8—TELL WHAT YOU KNOW

"Jesus of Nazareth, the son of Joseph."
John 1:45

Philip's description of Jesus sets off more than one alarm for those who know the details of Jesus' personal history. Jesus was raised in Nazareth; but he was "of" Bethlehem. It's true some mistakenly thought Joseph was Jesus' father. But the Bible is clear. Jesus was the son of God. He was born of a virgin; as we state in Gospel Story-arc presentations. So Philip's description of Jesus is incomplete and somewhat embarrassing. Why would John include it? Because that's what happened and John was committed to telling the truth. He also believed the rest of his gospel would show a more accurate picture of who Jesus is as the Christ, the Son of God.

Philip's story also shows how people grow in their awareness of who Jesus is. It reminds me of the story of the blind man that John tells chapter 9. The

Pharisees pestered the blind man, and then his parents, about what happened to him. They wanted to use the healing to prosecute Jesus for "falsely" claiming to be the Christ. So they said to the blind man, "Give glory to God. We know this man is a sinner" (9:24). But the blind man answered, "Whether he is a sinner I do not know. One thing I know; that though I was blind, now I see" (9:25). In other words, "I can't explain it. I just know what he's done for me. That's what I'm sharing with you!" The case of Philip and Nathanael is similar. Philip knew little about Jesus before sharing with Nathanael. So he just told what he knew.

This best practice of "Tell What You Know" is not meant to excuse inaccurate claims about Jesus; or diminish the importance of growing in knowledge about him. It simply points to not waiting to share until we know everything perfectly.

BEST PRACTICE #9—HAND PEOPLE OVER TO JESUS

"He brought him to Jesus."
John 1:42

After Andrew invited Peter, he handed him over to Jesus. Philip did likewise with Nathanael. The Samaritan woman followed suit with the townsmen. Why so quick to do this? Because they knew they could not convert anyone. Neither can we. That's not our job. Still, we may never know how or whether the seed of our witness sprouts and grows. But Jesus always knows, and he's the one in charge; therefore, we hand people over to him. The primary way is through prayer. Prayer reflects the heart-deep trust we have in the Lord, realizing that our witness is only one of the means the Lord may be using to bring people to himself. Our reliance on the Lord in this fashion will encourage us to keep on developing funneling skills and not to fall back on megaphone-practices as though everything depends on us.

BEST PRACTICE #10—USE STORY

"Come and see."
John 1:46

Many of us were taught to share the Gospel using logic, usually with an acrostic or some other clever form. Then we ask for a decision to believe in what Jesus did; not who Jesus is. It's not a bad approach to evangelism, but there is a problem. Actually, there are several problems, starting with how dismissive people are of our assumptions (e.g., that God exists, that the Bible is his Word, that he created all things, that we participated somehow in original sin, etc., etc...); and ending with how unwilling they are to embrace our logic. Our understanding of the Bible leads us to believe Jesus is the only way to salvation; they reject this.

This is where the value of using Jesus' larger story to share the Gospel comes in. Using Jesus' larger story to share overcomes the objections people have to our assumptions. You don't have to convince someone to believe that God exists, or that the Bible is his Word, or that he created the world, or that he is holy, etc., etc., for the story itself to break through to their hearts. Don't miss this—when God put the story together in his Word, he did not start with apologetics for his existence, his power, his authority as King over all, or anything else. He simply asserts, "In the beginning, God created the heavens and the earth...." The use of Jesus' larger story also overcomes the danger of people engaging with theology, but not with Jesus as a person. Theology is about ideas. Stories are about characters. When we use Jesus' larger story to share, we communicate he is a person people can relate to. He is not just an ideology.

Bonus 2

Gospel Story-arc®
Philosophy

The following statements describe the philosophy of the Gospel Story-arc® Project:

- Evangelism is the work of every Christian, not just the "professionals"; therefore, we believe every Christian should be trained on how to share.

- One goal of Gospel Story-arc evangelism training is to maximize the possibility of unsaved people hearing the gospel from a Christian friend.

- The ministry of evangelism must be bathed in intercessory prayer.

- Evangelism skills can be learned and improved; therefore, we train and coach others. And we continue to grow and learn from others.

- Showing someone how to evangelize is more powerful than just telling them; therefore, we practice what we teach.

- The sentence of death passed upon all has consequences for life now and for eternity; therefore, we practice gospel urgency.

- Salvation through faith in Jesus is more than relief from the penalty of sin; it includes the restoration of the relationships with God and others; self and the rest of creation.

- Unbelievers become believers in Jesus through a chain of communication events: Christians "sent" to "announce the good news", followed by unbelievers "hearing", then "believing in Jesus", and then "calling on him to be saved."

- The good news about Jesus is the larger story told in the Scriptures; therefore, gospel messaging extends beyond the creedal statements in 1 Corinthians 15:3-4: "...that Christ died for our sins, according to the Scriptures, that he was buried, and that he was raised on the third say, according to the Scriptures."

- The primary invitation to believe in NT gospel presentations asks people to believe in who Jesus is.

- Love for Jesus naturally accompanies heart-deep faith in him and who he is.

- The more one knows and appreciates the larger story of Scripture, the greater one's love for Jesus as a person and for the forgiveness that comes through him.

- Gospel messaging that prioritizes believing "that Jesus died for you" without explaining his larger story diminishes his place in the world and dangerously limits responses of love for him to those based solely on need-love.

- Evangelism is part of making disciples, not separate from it; therefore, we evangelize with the awareness that we have begun to make a disciple.

- Evangelism that prioritizes need-love responses to Jesus over appreciative-love is an Achilles' heel for making disciples.

- The brokenness of unbelievers in relation to others, self, and creation may be more salient to them than brokenness in relation to God.

- Gospel messaging includes hope and help for gaining victory over pain and suffering, death, and any other manifestation of evil as we navigate through life in this cursed realm.

- Unbelievers can be just as attracted to Jesus initially because of his impact on life now vs. the prospect of going to heaven someday.

- God designed human beings to process information of any kind using story elements.

- The use of story to share the gospel is the most effective way to secure attention, persuade, and guarantee shared meaning and retention.

- A well-designed summary of Jesus' story provides context and relevance for all claims we make about him; and about God, religion, sin, heaven, etc.

Bonus 3

Gospel Story-arc® Messaging and Worldview

Differences in worldview and cultural values may affect how well some people connect to gospel conversations, especially in relation to

- honor/shame

- innocence/guilt

- love/fear

Gospel Story-arc™ messaging adapts to this possibility, but not by changing the story that's told in Scripture. We simply use wording near the beginning to engage people from their point of view. For example, the messaging for Panel 5 states:

> Adam and Eve gave into the temptation and disobeyed. As a consequence, the four types of perfect relationships became broken. Where once there was honor, innocence, and love, now there was shame, guilt, and fear.

A gospel conversation that begins effectively might pause after this statement to ask:

> Which of these do you think is most devastating?

The answer you receive may uncover something you need to know about the person's worldview. Before moving on, you might use a follow up question to gain more insight:

Tell me more about why you think this?

As you continue sharing, you will be able to reference what you learn about the person's worldview into the messaging. For example, suppose you discover that the person holds a worldview of honor/shame. When you come to Panel 4, you could say:

> In response, God announced curses on the serpent, on Adam and Eve, and on the ground. The earth was no longer "very good." In addition to shame, sin and death became part of the world, as did pain, suffering, evil, and unbelief.

Then, in the messaging for Panel 5, you could say:

> The victory of "the offspring of the woman" indicates that he is also a Savior. He will rescue people on the side of the serpent from their shame (or from their sin and shame) and restore all things, including the four types of broken relationships. In the meantime, the serpent will do everything he can to deny the offspring of the woman space in the world.

Finally, in the Invitation to Believe, you could say:

> "Saved" means saved from judgment and shame, and rescued from the side of the serpent.

Adaptations to the worldview of the people we share with are just that—adaptations. They are not compromises, and they do not change the story of Jesus found in Scripture. Jesus' story, as told in Scripture, does indeed address each of the three categories of worldview, and it is the only story we are authorized to tell.

More Resources from the Gospel Story-arc Project

The Gospel Story-arc® Gospel Cube

The Gospel Story-arc® Gospel Tract
(4-panel, 3.5"w x 5.5"h)

The Gospel Story-arc® Community

Find these and more at **gospelstoryarc.org**

www.ingramcontent.com/pod-product-compliance
Lightning Source LLC
Chambersburg PA
CBHW080520090426
42734CB00015B/3119

9 781965 465011